OCC

By Lorne Cross

Copyright 2016 by Lorne Cross

Your World.

Your Choice.

The Mage stands with hands raised towards the sky and with feet firmly planted upon the earth.

A life lived in between the possible and the concrete.

This is the occult half-world of magick.

You know this place, and its power is familiar, because you have been here since the beginning.

TABLE OF CONTENTS

Magick with a 'K' - 6

Wield Magick - 10

Spell Casting - 19

Spellcraft - 35

Magickal Zones - 46

Temple of Spells - 58

Prosperity - 66

Protection - 78

Healing - 97

Attack - 112

Wizards Witches Everywhere - 119

Magick vs Magick - 126

The Toolbox - 133

Magickal Compost - 148

Why Magick? - 159

The Author - 170

MAGIC WITH A 'K'

The word 'occult' is a rather loaded one in our contemporary society, and conjures up a great many images ranging from satanic sorcerers, to stuffy armchair wizards, or wild witches. While all of those sorts of individuals fill our world, wielding magick both great and petty, there is a wider spectrum of occult forces at work in our world. Whether you are a curious beginner or a veteran practitioner, the fact that you have even read this far means that there is magick in your life, and that you want more. This book has been created to serve you as a guide and a tool on your journey through this magical life, please consider this my contribution to the enrichment of you as an occult force in your own right.

Everything that is real is real differently, and the source of information does not dictate what you do with that information. My job is to empower you, and nothing more. What you make of that power and what it makes of you… remains to be seen.

A man named Aleister Crowley said it best when he observed that magick is the science and art of causing change to occur in conformity to the will. In keeping with that maxim this work will use the 'magic with a K' spelling to differentiate between stage magic and the occult.

This is a slim magical text, a grimoire if you will, that has been written towards the purpose of providing modern seekers with a no-nonsense manual of magick.

In our modern world there is often a tendency to overlook the simple joy of magick in the pursuit of feeding our ego the self-styled image of ourselves as powerful sorcerers.

I want you to have cast a spell before we go any further. This is because the most important thing about magick is that you DO IT. We must dispense with the idea that you must go through considerable training and refined technique before you can cast effective spells. Such things help, tremendously, though are not pre-requisites for basic energy work. For those of you reading this book whom are already experienced with magick, consider this a back-to-the-basics act of goodwill. For those looking for darker work, don't worry, we will get to the badass black magick soon enough.

The purpose of this spell is for you to cast a blessing upon a person of your choice. Perhaps you will give that person good luck in their endeavors, or protection while they face obstacles, or simply an ambient good vibration that uplifts them as they go about their day. This is your spell so it is up to you to shape it how you will.

Think of someone important to you who is out there in the world. Hold in your mind the image of that person going through their day and visualize good feelings you have about them as a crackling mass of energy emanating from your lower chest, right at your solar plexus. As this energy pulses and vibrates think about the good memories you have of this person, and visualize those memories as thin strands of gossamer extending from you like a spider web that connect the two of you. Now begin to take notice of your breathing, and as you breathe in and out do your best to hold those memories and the crackling energy in your mind. Place your open hands over your solar plexus, and visualize the energy moving from you into your hands.

    Now move the energy with your hands over to the spider web of memories, and set the energy on the strongest strand, which is your strongest memory, like clothes on a clothesline or the seat of a ski lift. Once that is done keep breathing, and visualize that with every breath the energy makes its way across the strand like a lightning bolt that feeds the aura of your chosen person.

WEILD MAGICK

Did the spell work? Most likely yes, though generally with magick it is rather difficult to know for sure. Was it coincidence or magick that helped your friend give a great interview and land the job of her dreams? Perhaps it was both, and it was your spell that helped a possible outcome manifest as a tangible result. Magick is protean in that way, and is generally rather difficult to measure, predict, or prove. With all of our scientific prowess we humans have not yet been able to generate definitive proof that magick exists, though we have yet to definitively show that it does not exist, and that is something of a universal constant in the world of magick.

If you are going to seriously pursue a mastery of magick then you need to prepare yourself to let go of results, at least in the way that the scientific mind is trained to measure such things. The fact that you just cast a blessing spell and your friend just landed that dream job could very well be coincidence. Coincidence and probability manipulation are critical components of understanding how and why magick works, because the human mind thrives on the notion of causality. The principle that everything has a cause is one that I find to be at the core of magick.

    Imagine with me for a moment, that the whole of reality is a swirling tempest of energy, even if our perception of it is limited to the slowest vibrations. In this swirl of energy every effect has a cause, and those effects cause other effects, so on and so forth. The point being that everything is in motion, and magick, at its core, is about imposing our Will upon that motion. When you visualize reality in such a way you can easily see yourself as a swimmer in an ocean of light, or at least that's the visualization that works best for myself. The sorcerer, or mage, or wizard, or witch, or will worker, or whatever word you would like to use (my tastes change regularly) is a swimmer who can use their Will to manipulate and commune with this ocean of light. Magick is about motion, about transmuting potentiality into actuality, or more specifically manifesting outcomes.

    As you further internalize the idea that we are beings who exist in a realm of causality (for all we know) the more fluid your thinking and action will become in magical endeavors. The real artistry of magical endeavors is present in the observation of context forces, analysis of those forces, and resulting adjustment in your spellcraft. Let your imagination run wild, and visualize as much of your energy work as you can. Like the painter with brush on canvas you will find that your magick will be more powerful when you give it as much creative articulation as possible. Casting spells might not look like flashy movie special FX to the eyes of anyone else, but if that helps you do the deed with more potency, then visualize it as

Hollywood as you like.

Casting a spell, when you get right down to it, is a relatively simple act. It is a three-part movement of desire, knowledge, and will. Once you master those three elements you will be able to weave a tapestry out of reality according to your Will. If that's the case though, you might ask, why isn't everyone a reality shaping god-among-mortals?

There are two answers to this question, the first is blunt and could hurt someone's feelings, the second is more illustrative and workable for people who, like myself, aren't able to just be badass wizards overnight.

The first answer, the blunt one, is that not everybody is cut out to be an effective spell caster, because not everybody has what it takes.

Why doesn't everyone have what it takes? Good question, but not one I can answer. You could ask the same question about why everyone isn't a math whiz or a music prodigy. There is no clear reason as to why everyone isn't a magical virtuoso, and while I am a confident practitioner I wouldn't count myself in such esteemed company. That being said, I've only met a handful of people in my life who I'd call a virtuoso, or a prodigy, when it comes to spell casting, and if you are reading this book its likely that you aren't one either. That's because virtuosos aren't really out there buying books on the occult, because they can already do the thing at such a high level. The folks I've met whom I'd call virtuosos were also somewhat (ok dreadfully) uneducated in the magical arts. Kind of like the piano player who just lays hands on keys and makes the sweetest music, whereas folks like you and I have to work our assess off to make that same music. It is what it is, and I don't know why. Some people just have it and others don't.

The second answer is for those

who don't have that 'touch of the virtuoso' going for them. People like myself, who have found that learning and practice is how to best get things done. I think of using magick as kind of a metaphor for fencing, that sort of brutal and elegant swordplay from Europe. While any bloke can pick up a sword and swing it, not everyone has the courage, discipline, and work ethic to learn real swordplay. When you put in the time and the sweat (and maybe blood) you see that swordplay is a dance centered on the simple concepts of target acquisition and blade placement.

It takes a lot of work to transform yourself from being the person first picking up a sword and swinging it around wildly to the person who can parry, re-post, and coup de tat like a master swordsman. When I am working with people face to face that fencing metaphor seems to get through, possibly because I'm dancing around and waiving my finger, but still, I see the light bulbs go off in my student's brains. Spell casting is a simple concept, and easy to learn for just about any body, though achieving a true mastery of the magical arts is the result of making a monumental effort of study and training.

The magical thing about magick, at least in the occult eclectic tradition that we're inventing together, is that all training takes place out in the field (as it were). There is no inner sanctum where we listen to lecturers drone on and on. There is no podium from behind which the teacher can be safely removed from the students who paid good money to learn some magick and not listen to some blowhard talk for three hours. I believe that we have to get out there and DO magick. That is the only way we learn it, get better at it, and transform ourselves from the clumsy brute swinging a sword to the fencing master, minus the powdered wigs of course (unless that's your thing).

Look at how one simple spell has already catapulted us this far into forming an active engagement with the magical forces swirling all around us. One spell cast, many more to come, and from those yet more dynamic events will unfold.

Causality, always coming back to us isn't it?

The more experiences you have, the more spells you cast, the better you get at the whole endeavor.

Grab your journal and write down your experiences. It is important to keep a magical journal so that you can record your spells, and any other adventures you might have, so that you can go back later and investigate your progress. You will find that over time your relationship with magick will change, waxing and waning like the moon itself as your life goes through changes. As you go back through your experiences it is also possible that you will see patterns emerge. Perhaps you will discover that you go through phases yourself, and have entire months or years where most of your spells are benevolent, whereas you may have a time where hexing and cursing is the order of the day. By being able to go back and see your growth patterns you will be able to go into the next chapter of your life with more knowledge about who you are as a sorcerer, where you come from, and what you have already accomplished.

SPELL CASTING

This is where your magical journal continues to reveal its importance. Because we are casting spells from day one it is important to be disciplined about maintaining your journal.

Spell Casting is:

1. **Articulating Desire**
2. **Applying Central Theory**
3. **Employing Magical Will**

Once you learn those three things you will officially be the person who has both picked up a sword and has learned how to wield it with skill. Spell casting is Observing the context forces at work within the problem, Analyzing that information to determine the influence of those forces, and Adjusting your spell particulars to most effectively solve the problem and manifest your Articulated Desire. That, my friends, is masterful swordplay.

Let us now dive into the above

terms, and when you come back to the example hopefully the metaphor will have found an even deeper internalization for you.

Articulating Desire – This is the first and most critical step in the casting of an effective spell. Any time we are casting a spell it is because we are attempting to fulfill a specific desire. Any reason you can imagine that you'd have to cast a spell is rooted in desire. While other people actively hope, a sorcerer makes a decision. Casting a spell is the act of deciding, and the more explicit that decision is in your mind the more potent the results of your magical endeavor. This is true for two reasons, with the first being simply that knowing exactly what you want gives you some frame of reference, a perspective at it were, on the problem at hand.

If you, for example, want a better job and decided you're going to do something about it then before you even cast your spell there will be multiple elements in your life that can be put into play to help your spell be effective. You aren't likely to get a job without looking for one, or at the very least making yourself available publicly and energetically for a job to appear. Someone laying around on the couch all day watching TV and paying lip service to wanting a job doesn't really seem like the kind of person who is going to meet their spell halfway do they? I call it meeting your spell halfway, though more specifically it is creating a channel in which the waters of light can flow in order to manifest in your life.

There is the parable of the man who prays to god to grant him a lottery victory, and after it continues to not happen the man is angry with god. God responds by asking why the man couldn't have bothered to at least buy a ticket so that god could make it a winning one. You have to buy the ticket to win the lottery. You have to make yourself available for a new or better job in order to get one.

No amount of spell casting is going to yield a bountiful harvest if you don't plant some seeds yourself. Articulating the desire, initially, is about deciding what you want and making sure that you are open to the fulfillment of your desire. You have to meet the spell halfway.

The second reason to be as explicit as possible is that the more focused your statement of desire is the more tightly focused your spell will be, and thus the results. There are those practitioners that have a more "magick do as you will" kind of approach, where they loosely state their desire and even more loosely construct and cast their spells, and while this is a perfectly valid approach, the results tend to be as broad (even if no less potent) as the articulation of the desire and construction of the spell. In my thinking and experience, the more specific you are in the articulation of your desire, the more effective your spell will be, and the manifestation results will be more in line with your stated desire.

Applying Central Theory – Here we arrive at the crossroads, only instead of four possible directions think of it as a spherical crossroads, where an infinity of possibilities are available. It is upon this crossroads that most all conflicts of belief have their source. I call this step applying central theory because it is the step in which the sorcerer uses their chosen methodologies to construct the spell. The central theory of your magick is what, for the most part, defines how you choose to interact with the energetic realm.

Think of it as your chosen paradigm, belief system, magical tradition, or spellcasting style. Your central theory is the expression of how you live and work in this energetic realm, the way you work your magick. Another way to illustrate this would be to describe central theories as the 'mantles' that you wear when casting spells. There are many examples in the world of central theories, the most obvious being the religions of the world which teach that magick flows from gods or goddesses, or well known magical traditions such as Wicca, Thelema, Hoodoo, or Chaote Sigil magick. Each of these systems have their own way of interacting with energy, and the crafting of spells. While a hoodoo sorcerer might entreat Papa Legba to possess him and then imbue suit tie with power so that the bearer of the tie can successfully negotiate a complex business deal, that same problem could be solved by a Thelemite performing in a grand theatrical rite that focused both her energy and that of her allies on the suit tie, where a Chaos mage might create a sigil (a symbol cobbled together from the letters of the words used in the statement of intent, opinions vary on which letters, but usually the first of each word) to be drawn on the back of the tie.

All three approaches yield the

same result, but they all go about it in a different way because their belief systems shape how those practitioners construct their spells and interact with the world.

As practitioners of eclectic occult magick we are in a position to pick and choose what works for us from the existing religions and magical traditions of the world. We can also make up our own, quite literally as one invents works of fiction, and apply those methodologies to our spell casting. For example, when the creators of Hermetic magic were working in centuries past they did not have access to much of we do today, such as video games. Now, the Hermetic traditions generally center around theatrical rites in which the practitioners don costume pieces and take on the ritual persona of various magical characters within the recreation. By engaging in this complex ritual they go through a story, a transformation, and in so doing raise high levels of power that are shaped by the ritual towards the desired outcome.

It would be perfectly legitimate for an eclectic occult practitioner to apply this theatrical ritual idea to the playing of a specific video game. Perhaps taking a character through a level or specific stage of a video game could take the place of a more traditional ritual piece. In the mind and the magick of the eclectic occult sorcerer, the only different between Halo 4 and the Rite of Mercury (google it) is the power and meaning it holds for the individual participating in the ritual. Perhaps layered onto the video game rite would be myrrh incense, which is commonly associated with (paradoxically) grounding and engaging dreams. Another common element of spells in many traditions, especially Hoodoo and Wicca, is the ritual circle, so the video game rite could include that element as well. If the goal is, for example, to cleanse a house that is being plagued by angry ghosts or enemy spirits (perhaps even a curse laid upon anyone who resides there), then a circle of salt and iron could be used. Salt and iron are both able to function as 'energy disruptors' in the physical realm, and as such resonate with that disruption vibe in the magical realm, and so can be incorporated into spells for that sort of purpose.

As you can now see, we have used an eclectic occult approach to the spell construction, let us go back through and look at this central theory applied. The desire is to rid the house of negative energy patterns (fancy word for ghost, spirits, manifested curses, etc). The sorcerer lights a stick of myrrh incense with the intent of focusing their energy and opening their minds to full immersion in the game rite, and as the room fills with the scented smoke the sorcerer makes a circle on the floor using a mixture of iron filings and salt grains. The sorcerer cues up Halo 4 and selects a particularly engaging stage and then sits inside the circle. As the sorcerer plays through the stage they are focusing their Will on the game, envisioning the enemies they are battling on screen as the negative energy patterns they are banishing/dissipating. It is important to note here that in this example it is up to the sorcerer to select the game level and the difficulty, and this is a key element to consider.

All magick has a cost, usually of energy, time, and effort, but sometimes also one of sacrifice. Sometimes that is in the form of money, like paying someone else to cast the spell for you, a perfectly legitimate way to engage in magick. In ancient times, and in some modern traditions, animal sacrifice has been a way to supercharge spells of one kind or another. In this video game banishing rite example, the sacrifice is that you are cranking the difficulty up beyond your comfort level. If you breeze through the level then it might not challenge you sufficiently to raise enough energy for the spell to be effective. If you want to really blast that spell out at maximum power, then you should fight through the level at maximum difficulty. You might lose in the game, but stepping up to it is the part of the ritual that juices the spell and sends it out into the world.

Yes, I just compared playing Halo 4 to the more esteemed passion plays and theatrical rites of Hermetic, Thelemite, and various Mystery Schools.

For the occult sorcerer it is all about getting results using the beliefs and the tools that work best for the individual. I know plenty of practitioners that identify strongly with Star Wars, Jedi, and the Force. They are more likely to cast spells while thinking of the Force and gently waving their hands than they are to light a candle and repeat a spell mantra, or run naked through the forest while channeling the Horned God, or standing inside a complex symbol drawn on the floor in chalk and reciting ancient mystical formula spells.

Do what works for you, don't be afraid to experiment, and that is what matters. That being said, if you find yourself drawn to one particular tradition, strongly consider dedicating yourself to it, if the beliefs and central theory yield you empowerment. You are raising, shaping, and releasing energy, and that's it, nothing more and nothing less. Everything else is a matter of culture, belief, and perspective. There are no wrong answers in spell casting, only what works for you and what doesn't.

Employing Magical Will – Your Will (yes with a capital W) is the power within you that harnesses the energy, shapes it, and ultimately is your Decision Making Tool. Will is not a static trait, more the opposite, being something with a strength that waxes and wanes over time, depending on your internal landscape and your external environment. Magical Will is something you must work with in order to improve both its raw strength and your prowess in wielding it with mastery. Though it might sound cliché to some and tedious to others, I have found that mediation is the best metaphorical illustration of this concept in addition to being a prime tool for engaging and expanding your Magical Will.

While there are a plethora of mediation techniques, and accompanying philosophies, we will address the most basic style for the sake of clarity. Begin by sitting in a comfortable position, ideally with your legs crossed and slightly underneath you in the position that we all most commonly associate with mediation. Place your hands palm up or palm down on the tops of your knees. Later when you are doing magical work consider the sort of work you are doing and you will find that you will naturally gravitate more towards palms up or down depending on the work itself… sometimes it's a palms up kind of spell, sometimes it's a palms down kind of spell, that all depends on you and your connection with the spell.

Sit with your head up, face forward, shoulders squared, and back straight. There are a great many theories and schools of thought on body posture, especially how it relates to the magical energy that courses through our body, and it would be prudent for you to study a number of these ideologies so that you can build your personal framework for your mediation technique. Begin breathing, focusing your mind on filling the bottom of your lungs with air up to the tops, making it a deep breathing exercise instead of the shallow sort we get by with in our day to day lives. As you breath in and out the general idea is to clear your mind of all things, achieving what the Zen practitioners call 'no mind'. That simple goal is difficult in its own right, incredibly more so for those of us from a more 'Western' culture like America or the UK.

As you work with this mediation technique, you will find that there is a 'something' in your mind/body/spirit that you move within yourself to focus your body and make the repeated attempts to clear your mind. This 'something' is what you employ to wipe out the continuous stray thoughts that keep cropping up in your brain (the Zen folk call this 'monkey mind' because it won't cease its chattering). This 'something' is what you will find yourself using to maintain your physical position and posture without breaking the focus of the mediation. This 'something' will grow more powerful and simultaneously more fluid as you continue your mediation discipline. As you might have guessed, this 'something' is the seed that will blossom to become your Magical Will.

    Once you have taken notice of this 'something' in your mediations, you will begin to notice it as you form and cast your spells. It is the same 'something' that rises within you when you are lighting a candle and speaking the words of your spell, it is the 'something' that pushes back against people who may be trying to manipulate you, it is the 'something' that you used to draw upon when you were a child trying to play Jedi Knights or use Physic Powers. Once you become aware of your Magical Will then you are able to intentionally empower it, to be cognizant of its nuanced existence that permeates your being.

As you work, it is likely that your Magical Will shall take on a specific form within your imagination. Personally I experience my Magical Will as a gravitational force, while other practitioners I have encountered think of theirs as water, fire, and some a kind of solid light. It will be different for everyone, so whatever form it takes that feels natural to you is the one that will be most effective for you.

SPELLCRAFT

What we can consider the 'advanced' elements of spell casting is what I have chosen to think of as 'spellcraft'. It is in the 'craft' that the fine details of casting spells are employed. This craft element is somewhat unique to occult magick in that most spells you will find in other books are 'rotes', or static spells as it were. They are not flexible spells, and in this crazy world of ours being able to work some adjustments as the situations demands is a good thing. Here we will discuss the procedures of Observation, Analyzation, and Adjustment.

Observation - Nothing happens in a vacuum, and as such any problem you are engaging is going to be affected (causality again!) by a myriad of factors. Some of those will be internal to the problem itself, while most will be external to the problem. To cast an effective spell you will want to observe the problem. Naturally you will have already done this to a certain degree by virtue of the fact that you have decided to cast a spell as a solution. The idea is to observe on a deeper level, to see past the problem itself and look at the other forces that are at work. The more you cast spells and the more you practice this act of observation the more swiftly and completely you will be able to divine the internal and external forces at work.

Internal forces would be those that are already present within the problem. Observing, in a magical sense and in preparation for constructing and casting a spell, is about asking questions and seeking answers. Think of yourself as a detective, sifting through the energetic and temporal clues for any details that might help, hinder, or require adjustment spellwork on your part.

For example, let's say someone close to you has developed a horrendous drug habit in a short amount of time and you want to cast a spell to help him or her break out of it. First off, good on you for deciding to do something about it, and casting spells is something that only a few people will notice that you've done, so there won't be all that much additional strain on your relationship with this person, as they could be freaked out to know that you were doing work on their behalf. During the initial observation you see that your friend has rapidly developed a full-blown methamphetamine addiction.

Nothing happens in a vacuum.

You can cast a spell to make them stop wanting to smoke meth, and perhaps that spell could work with some degree of potency and longevity, but there could be factors internal to that person that are driving the problem. Perhaps there is an emotional or interpersonal need that is not being met, like a horrible break up or a death in the family, and by observing the situation you realize that helping this person get closure is the track to take with your spell, and that the meth isn't the most effective target.

Maybe your spell should be something that bestows emotional healing and mental clarity, and now that you have observed that you can analyze this detail and adjust your spell accordingly. Perhaps the person is not alone inside their bodies/minds/souls, and is suffering from some level of astral parasite, angry spirit, or a hostile curse. What that person needs is some spellwork that pushes away those energetic influences, and hopefully once that is done the person will have a better chance of recovering from the physical dependency.

External forces would be those that influence the problem while not being directly related to the problem. These are less obvious, but have the potential to be potent, as they inform the environment of the problem. An example would be the seasons, as summer carries with it a different energetic resonance than winter. Another could be the specific city or wild place in which the problem is occurring, as each corner of the world, whether rural or urban has its own resonance, a unique flavor if you will. Quite frankly there are some strange places in the world, and sometimes a problem that would not require a heavy-duty magical solution in London might be in dire need of magical intervention on the African savannah.

A keen example of that would be a sick individual in need of care. If that person were in New York City, for example, they would generally have access to a modern hospital. If you were casting spells to help that person recover you might be enchanting the patient so that they would be "red tape proof" and experience a swift trip through the heavily bureaucratic medical industry. Or you might cast mental clarity spells on the doctor who sees the sick person so that the doctor has a much higher probability of diagnosing the illness properly.

If the sick individual was on a trip with you in the jungles of Mexico, without access to hospitals or airlift, then consulting with the local healer would be the best move, as they would be connected with the land, the spirits, and likely have a magical (even if combined with physical) solution. If there is no local healer, and you were on your own, then it would be up to you to seek out that assistance from the spirits of the jungle, perhaps while casting spells to stimulate the person's immune system or to extract the energy of the illness and perhaps deprive it of its ability to thrive.

Ultimately observing is about extending your awareness over, under, and into the problem, so that you can get as close to a full spectrum picture. It is about asking questions, about looking deeper, and doing your best to remember that all of those forces in play will be affected by your spell. Observation is about not only determining what forces are at work within the problem, but also accepting and being aware of the fact that your spell's affect will ripple out and touch all of these forces in some way.

Analyziation – Those ripple effects bring us to the analyzing stage, where you carefully weigh and inspect each of the forces at work within the problem. Again, the more you do this, the more you cast spells, the more swiftly and accurately you will be able to work through these steps. Eventually you'll be casting spells in the blink of an eye, because you've already done the work. I have developed a simple framework that I employ for this step, and over time had refined it to what I'll call "Magickal Zones", included in a chapter all their own, for quick reference. Feel free to skip ahead and read about the zones before returning to this chapter for a more informed reading of the Adjustment phase.

Though this list might seem daunting at first, consider how easily you operate a computer, once thought to be one of the most complex machines in existence. Computers certainly ARE incredibly complex machines, but through practice and a basic understanding of how they work the average person is able to operate them with relative ease. In this way the computer is a very easy illustration of what our goals are as magical practitioners.

As eclectic occultists we are seeking to be somewhat more knowledgeable, versatile, and effective with both symmetrical and asymmetrical problem solving methods. While I am not at all looking down my nose, as it were, at the common witch, I would liken them more to 'computer users' as opposed to being programmers, hackers, engineers, etc. As eclectic occultists we are keen to delve deeper into the 'computer' to achieve a mastery of both the hardware and the software, and in so doing become 'mega-users'. We build our own computers, write our own code, create our own systems. These 'magickal zones' are my framework for taking that step towards being a mega-user, as it were.

Adjustment – Once you have fully analyzed the problem and determined what zones are at work and in what degree, now comes the time to make changes in your spell so as to make it as effective as possible. It all sounds complex and technical, and at first it is, though as you work with magick on a regular basis the more routine all of these steps will become. The more 'second nature' such observation and analyzation become the more swiftly you will be able to move through all of the steps. That being said, patience is a powerful tool in and of itself, when the situation allows for it.

Perhaps as you observe and analyze you discover that your spell requires more or less of a particular zone, and through observation you determine what change suits the spell best.

Let us consider an example from my own past. A friend of mine was working as a healer in his local community, which was comprised of a mix of pagan identified people (some Wiccan, some less specific) and Vodoun practitioners. He was effective in his charge, and people often came to him for energy work and advice. He in turn came to me when he became convinced that he was suffering from a massive spirit parasite infestation, complete with sudden failing health, nightmares, and a sense of his energy being 'shorted out' when trying to perform his healing work.

As I observed the problem I could tell that he was indeed being chewed on by parasitic spirits, though as I delved deeper I gained a sense that they had been placed upon him, as if driven by the will of another. I then adjusted my spell to attack not the parasites, but shifted to a different spell entirely as I worked to create a counter-curse. I informed my friend that while he was infested it was due to a curse that had been laid upon him, and as I worked against the curse itself his personal energy began to return so that he could do the work of healing himself from the parasites.

As we move through the steps in creating the spell we may discover that the spell we initially thought to cast has been transformed by the problem into something different and yet vastly more effective.

MAGICKAL ZONES

As we analyze the situation we apply the magical zones to enable us to have a working model for dissecting and engaging the problem. We determine what zones are in play, and to what degree, and as we become more attuned to having a magical zone mentality the more swiftly and effectively we will be able to apply the framework. As with any other eclectic approach to occult magick, you may find that you desire to break these nine zones down even further, to create an even more complex flowchart of forces at work within the problem, and that is your prerogative. For the sake of this book I will present the zones that I have found to be the most comprehensive and powerful in my own magical journey through life.

Connection – We have all heard it said over and over that everything is connected, though it is internalizing a deep understanding of this interconnectedness that can empower us to tinker with those metaphorical strands in the great web that binds us all together. This zone is most easily understood as awareness of the connectivity within not just things, but ideas, even symbols. Sympathetic magick, where a physical item is used as a dynamic symbol of something else, is rooted in the zone of connection. The same can be said for Contagious magick, in which some item of the spell (or energy pattern) comes in contact with the target of the spell in order to transfer the spell, as it were. To put it another way, anyone who wears symbols of religion or magick (crosses, pentacles, ankh, etc) is drawing upon the symbolic connection between the physical instance of the symbol and the ideas and energies associated with that symbol. There is also connection between places, and so this zone plays heavily into spells having to do with travel.

For example, you may be moving from one city to another, but those places are connected by the fact that they are in the same nation, on the same continent, upon the same planet, in the same physical reality, so on and so forth. The idea being that everything that exists, from people, to places, to symbols, to ideas, are connected in some way. Learning to achieve an awareness of those connections, and then filter out those connections until you have a firm grasp upon the 'thread' you are seeking, will enable you to fully analyze and adjust in your spellcraft.

Probability - The 'likelihood' of something happening, or not happening, or becoming, or not becoming, can be manifested into a tangible energy that can be manipulated by the practitioner. Like the Law of Thermodynamics, which states that heat is lost, has been constructed by human beings as both a tool of measurement and an idea that informs how we interact with the world. As we begin to internalize the understanding that 'outcomes' are perfectly fluid until the very moment they become 'actualities', we can develop constructs to empower us to manipulate those outcomes and apply our Will towards our desired actualities.

Let us consider an example of probability magick in a familiar setting. Perhaps you are at home and using a knife in the kitchen to cut a piece of fruit, and the knife slips. For a moment there are a plethora of possibilities, many of them involving you getting cut and others involving the knife simply shearing off more fruit than you wanted or biting into the cutting board. Call it small magick if you want, but I absolutely have blessings placed upon my kitchen for good food and safety. With an enchantment intended provide safety I have done magical work in this zone to affect a reduction in the probability of accidents. If you need a bigger example then consider charms placed in your car to avoid collisions, symbols etched into armor to keep warriors alive, or blowing on dice before you throw them at the gambling table. When we witness that there is a deep pattern at work in the swirling energy of chance and mathematical decay, we can work with that pattern, inviting a sort of guided chaos into our spellcraft.

Life Force – My sense of this zone is two-fold, with the first being an awareness of the spark of life within all living things, the second being the burning intent within the subject in question, whether conscious or unconscious. The spark of life is my way of communicating that lightning in all living things, the animus if you will, that holds us on this side of the mortal coil. All living things have electricity coursing through them in one form or another, and it is that inner lightning of which I speak. This ties heavily into the zone of connection, in that all living things in one sense share a single lightning bolt, each sharing in a tiny spark of that one bright source. To sense and be aware of the sparks at work within your problem is critical, not only because what you do will affect the world and life forms around you, but there is also their burning intent to contend with.

I call it 'burning intent' as my own meager way of describing that ineffable quality in life that pushes it to strive onwards. Another way to think of it would be 'purpose', because that purpose will have a momentum all its own, which could work for or against your magick. Life is never benign, and so you must consider life in your magick. Life will strive to fulfill its purpose, to manifest its intent, especially if you are dealing with one or more conscious/sentient beings that are aware of their purpose. Being aware of this momentum will inform your spellcraft.

Consciousness – This zone is more about you than it is others, and how you are relating to the inner and exterior worlds at work in your own life. Your state of mind, as it were, is critical in spellcraft, and as such must be taken into consideration when in the analyzation and adjustment phases. Your emotions could be getting the better of you, or you may find that you haven't had enough sleep, or your thoughts may be moving so fast and insistently that you are unable to properly focus your full attention on the spell. Running a personal diagnostic of your own mind is something that takes practice, though with regular meditation and experience you will find that it becomes more and more of an automatic response.

While the above aspect of this zone may sound very clinical, it is also part of any endeavors involving altered states of consciousness. Some acts of magick, especially those involving spirits or astral projection, rely heavily upon the practitioner being able to fully immerse themselves in the spell. If you are meditating and undergoing an astral projection endeavor, being able to maintain that focus and connection with your work is paramount. To put it another way, it will be very difficult to astrally project your consciousness into another realm if you had too much coffee or are unable to filter out the cacophony of voices insisting that you give attention to your phone, television, or unattended chores. All of the above also applies to the other sentient beings that may be present in your problem scenario, and their consciousness, or at least what you can sense of it (employ your understanding of connection) should be taken into account.

Energy – Let us acknowledge the idea that all things are energy, moving at different vibrations, and then put the notion aside. For the phases of spellcraft we are seeking an awareness of the specific energies at work within the problem at hand. While energy, in its purest form, has no resonance beyond simple radiance, we as human beings are unlikely to have the capacity to sense energy in such a primal state. We are more apt and attuned towards energy that has been shaped towards some purpose, even if one occurring in the natural world. When you are observing and analyzing a problem you would be using this zone to determine what energy is at work and the resonance of that energy. The resonance, or flavor if you will, of the energy will inform you of how it may or may not factor your spellcraft. With this zone you are reaching out with your senses, savoring the energetic soup that is the local reality, and making adjustments based on what you find.

Perhaps one kind of magick would be better suited to the environment, or other spells may already be at work and should be taken into account, or spirits may be present.

For example, let us imagine that you have been asked by a friend to rid their house of an unwanted presence. Depending on the 'vibe' of the house, the energy moving within it, and perhaps even the presence itself, you could adjust your spells accordingly. A sprawling Victorian mansion has different architecture than an urban studio apartment, and as such their energies will be different, so too would your spellcraft in such a place. It would be prudent to make the effort to give at least a few hours of study to architecture and the art of Feng Shui, as we are modern humans living in a modern world, and the way we build our structures directly affects how energy moves within them. This is more readily apparent in places like forests or the open ocean, where the primal energy has been less altered by human influence, and being in the modern urban environment requires the practitioner to put in somewhat more effort to filter through all of the various energies that are in play.

Spirit - There are, generally, two schools of thought when it comes to magick, from a traditional standpoint. There are those people and traditions that insist magick comes in the form of powers and gifts that are granted to the practitioner by other beings (spirits, gods, angels, etc) and then wielded by the Magical Will. On the other side of the issue there are those people and traditions who believe that magick comes from within the individual themselves, and that their power is their own, to be shaped by their will and hurled into the world.

I believe, through my own study and experience, that the truth lies somewhere in the middle, if not fully in both camps.

Many powerful traditions both new and old, including but not limited to Wicca, Vodoun, Santeria, Hermeticism, and Kabbalah draw much, if not all, of their power from 'others'. In those traditions the general practices is to make contact with the 'other' and then after some form of supplication, enticement, bargain, or command, a boon of power is granted. The practitioner channels that power, shapes it to his or her will, and then releases it into the world in the form of a spell.

Those who believe that power

comes from within, in my experience, generally do not work with 'others', hereafter referred to generally as spirits. They visualize a wellspring of energy emanating from within themselves, to be shaped and cast with skill and will.

TEMPLE OF SPELLS

The name of this section is a play on words, though one that I feel holds an element of power worth considering. I am about to lay out a basic template for spell creation that can be applied to any magical activity. As such, I choose to see this formula in my personal practice as a 'temple' from which I operate. A temple is a sacred space, one that can provide defense as well as succor, and be a stronghold from which to base.

It is intentional that I use a temple metaphor as my spell creation foundation, because in the heat of the moment, or even for carefully considered magicks, having this mental/inner temple empowers you greatly. Think about all of the simple mathematical formulas you have internalized, and the act of 'doing math in your head' is something that can help you move through your day-to-day life.

This is operating off of the

same broad idea, that with an internalized foundation you can use the particulars of occult spellcraft to visualize, construct, and cast complex and effective spells without having to pause to crack open a dusty tome of spells or flip through the pages of some Book of Shadows. Will having such books available help you? Most assuredly, and when you are able to layer any additional empowerments into your spellcraft you are encouraged to do so. The point is that you don't need anything but the formula, the temple as it were, to create effective magick.

You will find that all of my spells are presented as being part of one of four meta spell groups, those being Prosperity, Protection, Healing, and Attack. As with the magical zones it is possible that you may find it more appropriate for your work to create additional spell groups, and the goal of my Temple Template is for you to have the tools to do so.

There are many areas of magick

that are not touched on in this book, and that is because from my perspective they can all be placed in one of the four major groups. Spells that pertain to things like 'love' and 'fertility' strike me as Prosperity spells, just like those for 'gambling' and 'money'. For spells that pertain to things like 'beauty' and 'longevity' or 'childbirth' I would place under Health. The spells that you might associate with 'theft' and 'missing persons' I would place under Protection, as I would with anything pertaining to the 'evil eye' or 'counter-curses'. My spell group Attack would hold under its title anything that involved aggression, so 'hexes' and 'curses' would find their way there. The act of using magic to dominate or persuade someone would be in Attack, while generally the defenses against such spells would be in protection.

The 'black magick variant' section is included in some spells listed below to present the reader with alternative spell methodologies that would allow for more profound magical attacks and counter-attacks. I have included this element in some of the spells not only to inform the reader, but also to differentiate between what I consider 'black magick' and 'attack magick', as I believe that they are very different.

The difference is in the intent and outcome, and you will see that illustrated as you read through the list of spells, especially the Attack spells. I believe in a balanced approach to magick, and there are times in one's life where simple attack and defense magick is not enough, and you find yourself calling upon the darker parts of your power. It is not for me to judge, or to place any sort of value on what you might do with this newfound power and knowledge. I believe that 'magical violence' and 'magical malevolence' are rather different, founded on intent and shaped by the spells that are cast. My job is to teach you magick, as best I can, from these meager pages. As such, you need to know some black magick, because at some point in your life you may find that it is what best suits a given situation. We human beings are not without malice, and at times even good people find that malevolent actions are useful.

For others it is possible that your job in this life is to be a full-tilt black magick practitioner, and so be it, it is my job to give you the tools to be whatever you are going to be and to help you be as effective as possible in that role. As practitioners of Vodoun might say, I 'serve with both hands', and so work with magick from a great many spectrums of what might be considered 'good' or 'evil' or 'positive' and 'negative'. Be the occult force you empower yourself to be.

As a final note, before we begin discussing the spell template and spell groups, remember that study is important. Not just study of this book of course, but of as many other cultures and traditions as possible, because it is through this study that you will find the pieces of 'occult tech' that will work best for your individual practice. This isn't about cultural appropriation so much as it is about an eclectic approach to occult magick, using the parts of other's work that is best suited to you personally, and growing from there to form your own inner culture and outer traditions.

The Spell Temple

1. **Function** - the spell name is the purpose
2. **Context** - origins of spell
3. **Materials** - required ingredients or verse
4. **Execution** - step by step instructions

All spells in the eclectic occult system can be broken down into those four components, and the idea is that you can take this template and use it to build your own Temple of Spells. You are also invited to seek out other spells from whatever source you chose and break them down with this simple formula. There are many books and manuscripts detailing literally thousands of spells from across history and into the contemporary world, so you will have your work cut out for you.

Now that we have laid out the template for spell creation, please allow me to present you with a sample of my own Temple. I collect grimoires and occult texts, across a multitude of cultures, though I generally find that I favor a more 'pagan' magical approach. That is to say, I often find myself resonating with the use of elements typically associated with witchcraft, like candles, herbs, stones, and blood. While I do in fact work with sprits from time to time, I will focus on presenting a majority of spells that do not incorporate direct contact or communion with spirits. Partially because I believe that armed with this book you will be able to engage those spirits on your own, and also because there are already so many other books that are filled with pages upon pages of workings with spirits.

    I shall, however, include a number of spells that will directly draw upon the resonances of certain spirits, as a way of illustrating the fact that you can work with 'spirit energy' without directly interfacing with the conscious and actualized being itself.

PROSPERITY

Dice for Cash

In the dice game of craps the shooter (he or she who rolls the dice) can make what is called a pass line bet. If the roll yields a 7 or an 11 the pass line bet wins. This spell is intended to draw upon the 'fast money' vibe inherent in gambling, especially the game of craps, as it is the most widely known dice game and most commonly associated with the ideas of Lady Luck, Mama Fortuna, and a great many spirits of luck, chance, and prosperity. The ideal outcome is a windfall resulting in swift amounts of liquidity for yourself or the person for whom you are casting the spell.

Materials – pair of dice, green candle, gold glitter

Execution – Carve symbols of prosperity, wealth, and money into the green candle. Roll the dice until they come up 7 or 11, and once they do leave them where they fell. Light the green candle and drop wax onto the dice until they are completely encased. While the wax is still warm take a pinch of gold glitter and visualize filling that glitter with your intent, in this case the desire for quick cash, and then sprinkle the glitter over the dice.

Black Magick Variant – Carve symbols of scarcity, poverty, and ruin into a black candle. Roll the dice until they come up snake eyes, and then encase them with the wax. Instead of throwing glitter throw salt upon the warm wax, symbolic of 'salting the fields'. All of this would be done with the conscious intent for the person you are casting the spell on to suffer a swift loss of cash/liquidity (perhaps a stocks crash or broken water heater).

Web of Fortune

There is a saying, that the golden money spider weaves a web of riches. So too is there another saying, that if you wish to live and thrive, let the spider stay alive. Spiders do indeed weave their webs, and into those deathtraps fall the usual pests that we must otherwise find ourselves contesting with. We associate webs with nets, and nets with bounty, though as (generally) we are people from a capitalist society we must associate winning and losing with our economics (like the spider and the bug caught in the net), and so we imagine Fortune as a food chain of sorts. This spell relies upon those innate iconic vibrations, in addition to (for those so inclined) a definite connection with the spirit of Grandmother Spider, whom holds a web that provides for her supplicants.

Materials - red paper, gold or silver ink, saucer made of metal or clay (cheap wares make for cheap spells - this is key!)

Execution - Draw a picture of the spider in its web, whether this is more of a bullseye style drawing or something more labyrinthine, and then place the picture in a corner of your living space with a saucer underneath it. Toss a few coins onto the saucer, filled with your intent for a more lasting and profound 'web' of fortune to encompass your life. Invite the spider energy (or explicit spirit) into your life, and once a week (or whenever you feel like the spider had directly come through for you), put up another offering. Naturally the more potent your offerings the more energy poured into the spell, and the more potent the overall (and long term) results. The key here is to make continuous offerings of energy, and when you are able do increase the denomination of the cash you've placed in the saucer (if not the physical amount, as that would become cumbersome over time).

Bathing in Wealth

In many cultures and traditions the herb basil draws opportunity towards those who bear its physical presence, in the form of leaf or scent, expressly with financial gain as a focus. While to the modern sensibility a 'ritual bath' could be look askance upon, that very act of physically 'bathing in symbolic wealth' is a very powerful one, now more than ever precisely because it is seen by the contemporary mind as odd. The goal here is to steep the physical body in both the spell components and the energetic resonance of financially specific opportunity, so that one may go out into one's day (or night) with a tremendous empowerment towards success.

Materials – fresh basil, ritual vessel, water, bath or basin

Execution – Chop up a large bunch of basil in order to release the natural oils present within the plant, do so with intent towards the spell being cast as one works with knife and plant. Gather herb cuttings in your ritual vessel, anything that you have determined to be participant in the ritual and capable of holding boiling water. Pour boiling water over the cuttings and let steep until the water is cold, ideally the caster would continuously pour energy into the mixture as it cools to further power the spell. Pour the basil mixture into a hot bath (or hot water in modest basin) and soak in the ritual bath. You are literally and magically soaking in wealth and opportunity laced energy (think zone of probability mixed with zone of life force). Once you have soaked for 10 to 20 minutes remove yourself from the bath and allow yourself to air dry. If you have no bath and are going with the basin method this will be all the easier. Walk with confidence into your next opportunity encounter, be it a job interview, stock trade, promotion discussion, raise review, trade deal, or act of gambling, etc.

Avocado Money

The avocado is a delicious food item, rich in proteins and good fats, in addition to being a tasty green food. Because of its color it is commonly associated with energy patterns of bounty, though because of its fickle ripeness there is a reminder present of its fleeting boon. The idea here is to use the avocado as a key component in a spell that embodies the "make hay while the sun is shining" mentality of grasping bounty and opportunity when it is presented, before it is too late. There is a deep connection to the land present in this food, one easily seen due to the plant's color and earthy flavor, and the avocado draws the energy of 'bounty' to it. If you think about what most of us spend money on, it is food and drink and shelter and comfort, which can all be seen as 'bounty', and so while this spell may not yield the piles of cash that some of the others do, it brings into your life the kind of abundance that last beyond a dollar here and a dollar there. This spell is simple in its execution, and may seen like physical labor and superstition, but this is deep magick, and you will feel its effects for years to come.

Materials - Fledgling avocado tree

Execution - Plant a fledgling avocado tree and eat the very first avocado that grows from it. Clean and dry the pit so that it can be used as a bounty charm, to be carried on the person or prominently placed in the home. Avocados from this tree can be given to others to spread the bounty energy.

Black Magick Variant - Fortune is fickle, and our wealth can be here today and gone tomorrow. This is much like the avocado, in that it can be perfectly ripe and delicious today, but tomorrow it can be foul indeed. To foul the bounty energy that may be filling an individual's life you would harvest an avocado from your tree and wait until it has become foul. Fill the rotten thing with your intent to destroy the bounty energy patterns in the life(s) of your target(s) and place the avocado as close to the targets as possible. Depending on your circumstances this could be as overtly aggressive as hurling it against the front door of their house or more are more subtle approach such as burying it where they live or smearing the rotting thing across something they own and hold dear.

The Silver Plan

For many peoples around the world the Moon's light, especially on the New Moon and Full Moon phases, resonates with (in an obvious symbolic way) energies of fortune, wealth, and prosperity. The Moon is an enigmatic heavenly body, so too are the various spirits and deities associated with it. Not to mention the various bits of folklore about the devils and monsters that roam under the silver glow, with purposes both bloody and laden with possible gain for those bold enough to claim the boon. The Moon's light is swift, and moves with a kind of piercing grace that has mystified human beings since we first glanced up at the night sky. This spell captures that quicksilver energy, harnesses the protean light towards financial goals of great risk and great reward. Tread carefully with this spell, because while success can be tremendous there is always the chance that fortune's favor can shift and leave you holding the proverbial (and in this case literal) bag. This is a spell for those who are about to launch new endeavors, who seek to harness the quicksilver power of the moon to act as the nitro-fuel that ignites the enterprise towards elevated heights of success.

Materials – freshly acquired credit card, outdoor altar or ritual platform, new or full moon in a clear enough sky to get lots of moonlight

Execution – If you have a new business or otherwise entrepreneurial endeavor that you wish to infuse with tremendous additional power, in addition to liquidity, keep an eye on the moon cycles. Prior to a new or full moon (the choice of which is up to you, though I personally suggest new moon for brand new businesses and full moon for established endeavors) secure yourself a new credit card. The maximum amount doesn't have to be all that much, just enough to warrant a new plastic card to be sent to you (so even $50 is good, but as with all magick, the more you risk the more you stand to gain). Take the card and place it on an outdoor altar or any suitable surface otherwise consecrated towards this purpose. Let the card bathe in the moonlight as you fill the card with your intent and desire. For those of you working directly with Moon spirits or deities make the appropriate additional offerings or supplications. Once the card has spent the evening in the moonlight, being moved as needed throughout your all-night vigil to make sure it is bathed in moonlight the entire evening, it will be ready. Take the card and spend as needed to grow your business, empowered by the magick of your ritual and the moon. When not in use keep the card away from sunlight, in a bag or pouch, to keep the Moon's blessing fresh and undiluted by the Sun's influence.

PROTECTION

Witch's Ladder

I have chosen to place this spell in the protection chapter, though I would argue that with a shift of intention this particular spell (or its variants) could function for just about any goal. I am a proponent of knot magick when I am working with people 'in person' and would recommend this style of working to anyone. I find that the act of choosing the rope/string, determining number and type of knot, and intent makes this spellcraft tool something of a 'multi-tool', the 'Swiss army knife' of magick as it were. As humans we are physically oriented beings, and as important as knots were to us in the times leading up to our complacent modern age, I find this methodology of magick to be one of the more potent sorts. This spell is called the Ladder because the idea is that nine knots that are tied into the rope resemble the utilitarian rope ladders of common culture. Nine is a powerful number (like the idea of nine runes and nine realms in Nordic magick) and this spell encourages the caster to focus their energy and intent into the spell as they tie one knot after another. Some witch's knots are simple overhand knots, others are much more complicated, and I suggest you study knotwork so that you are able to find the physical knot that works best for you. Needless to say if you choose to make knotwork an integral part of your magical practice (as I have) then you will likely end up using different knots for different spells and resonances, and this is yet another way in which this spell is so immanently versatile.

Materials - length of rope, skill at tying at least one sort of knot

Execution - For the purpose of this book I am including this spell as one of protection. Knots, especially when tied with specific intent, are exceptionally powerful at dissipating incoming energy. If the energy is unwanted (like an enemy spell or some ailment, curse, or otherwise), the knots re-route and dissipate the energy as it comes into the life of the practitioner (the creator of the ladder). This spell can be used in two ways, when it comes to protection. The first is that when the practitioner suspects or has confirmed that an enemy hex present then as the practitioner creates the ladder (nine knots in one piece of rope) they are pouring their intent of protection and shielding into the knots so as to dissipate the incoming hostile energy patterns. The second is to remove an existing hex or curse, something already 'on' the practitioner. With the second it could be much harder to stay focused, to summon up the energy, and this is a classic "contested spell" scenario. The only thing to do at this point is push through it, and keep tying the knots, in fact to allow the tying of the knots to become your focus will enable you (possibly, likely even if your meditation discipline is honed) to fight past those distractions (manifestations of the curse as it protects itself) and dissipate the spell and defend yourself.

Black Magick Variant – Much the same theory, only in this case you are attacking your target. You may be tying the knots to 'bind' them, be it to your will or to simply remove them from your 'chess board' as it were. Perhaps you mean to kill them, and are tying knots that each constrict the organ functions within a target, causing pain and possible eventual death. Or maybe you are simply looking to draw away any fortune and goodwill that maybe en route to the target. It's all about intent at this point, focused and flavored by the spell you are casting and the physical knots you choose. You may choose to bury the ladder on the property where the target works, lives, or frequents. This could be done also if you are targeting a specific group or building, much the same as if you were attempting to lay protection or healing upon them. Burying the ladder after tied is a potent act, whether it is for healing, protection, or attack.

Shield of Iron

Iron is such a famously potent substance for dispelling malevolent energy that such references are prevalent even in the blandest of contemporary consumer culture stories. There is a powerful truth to most depictions of iron as a sort of 'anti-magical' material, though that is only part of the picture. Our beliefs empower things, and the story of iron and its magical properties has been told since the Iron Age itself. That kind of cross-cultural momentum serves to empower iron to the point that even items that have a percentage of iron and aren't even pure can still be employed towards great purpose. When our beliefs as practitioners, fueled by our Will, are able to 'flow with the current' of conventional reality, then our work can become that much more potent. This spell isn't as much about a specific item, but the substance of iron, the essence as it were, and how you can work with that essence using whatever physical item that works best for your needs. Iron yields an 'active' and 'dynamic' sort of energy to your spellcraft, and so protection spells that incorporate iron tend to be somewhat more aggressive in nature then those cast using wood, stone, or wine.

Materials – Items made of iron, such nails, horseshoes, beads, knives, spears, swords, treated iron pipes from a hardware store, etc

Execution – The spell variants for this are endless, though some examples follow. For a basic wearable shielding spell an iron nail can be worn as a necklace, carried in the pocket (wrapped in leather for extra punch), or even tied to your hair if your style is of sufficient length. To dispel a curse upon your or perhaps rid yourself of negative energies (or spiritual parasites) a ritual bath could be created by tying a nail to the top of the faucet so that as the water comes out it touches the nail, allowing you to 'soak' in the liquid that has been infused with a malignant/malevolent dispelling energy. If you wish to help someone else with a spell, then using an iron knife, slashed in a violent striking motion as you face each of the cardinal directions (east, west, south, north) would be the foundation for a spirit banishing or curse lifting spell. For protection of the home install a wrought iron gate or window guard, installed by you personally (and not a handyman) so that your intent can fill the structure and carry the protection over the entire home. If you are encountering a particularly entrenched parasite, curse, or other complex and powerful malevolent force, it is possible to purchase an iron bed frame. Sleeping on a bed with an iron frame will allow you to pull the magic of the iron to form a case all around you, allowing for the enemy powers to be dispelled and to keep you defended while you heal and recover.

Hematite Counter-Curse

This stone is imagined by many cultures to have the natural ability (a tendency some would say) to draw negative, malignant, and malevolent energies into itself. Because of this cultural momentum of belief and (in my experience) actual function, hematite is used by many healers to draw out the 'bad juju' that causes some illness and that is present in the aftermath of spiritual assaults and active curses. The first part of this spell is actually identifying that you or someone you are working with has been hexed, cursed, spiritually attacked, or otherwise harrowed by malevolent forces. Often we jump to conclusions and think we have been cursed when in truth we have experienced a string of bad luck, a series of unfortunate coincidences, or suffered a spate of ill fortune or bad health. It's a tough world out there, and sometimes the not great stuff just happens to us thanks to time, chance, and our own mistakes. However, sometimes the coincidence is just a little too perfect, or the bad luck has a dark sort of vibe to it that feels laden with intent, or that pain in our side is just too sudden and unexplained. In my experience getting a second opinion is a good first move if you think you've been the victim of a spiritual attack or the target of a curse. When we are all wrapped up in dark energies it can be tough for us to be fully objective, and sometimes even the most badass wizards need help. Self-diagnosis might be your only option, in which case I suggest taking the iron bath and THEN going for the hematite counter-curse, just to make sure you're getting everything. This spell is all about drawing out and collecting all the nasty stuff that is clinging to you, in a sort of 'scorched earth' capacity, so be prepared to take a long nap afterwards, or at the very least have some time to meditate and collect yourself before being too active, because this kind of energy doesn't like to let go without a fight.

Materials – A buddy who can perform the spell with you is ideal, but if you are alone you obviously will do what you need to do. Several pieces of hematite, the more raw and un-machined the better. For most of us getting raw hematite on short notice is pretty tough, so if you have to run down to your local new age shop or touristy rock shop to buy several pieces of polished hematite just buy a few extra to make sure you have enough. There's no science or occult secret to divining how much bad juju any particular piece of hematite can hold, but trust me, you'll know when its full and that's when you need to swap it out for a fresh one. Also bring a container that has been prepared, with your intent and magical will, to be a holding area for bad juju. Personally I have an old cigar box that I place the stones in, nothing special carved or drawn in it, the box just feels right to me and that's how I know it will do the job. So much of this stuff is following your instincts and letting your ego sit back long enough for your senses to guide you effectively.

Execution – Ideally you would strip naked for this bit of ritual magick, so that you can get a full treatment, though if that's not doable with your buddy of choice then do what you can (and then go find more a down-to-spell buddy for next time). You or your casting partner (if you brought a buddy) run the hematite across as much exposed skin as you have time for, so ideally the stone(s) will pass across every major part of your body. As each stone fills up with the bad juju place it in your special container and pick up where you left off with a fresh stone. Once the whole body has been treated (and feel free to do the whole thing a few times until the stones don't feel like they are picking anything up anymore) then dress yourself and dispose of the full hematite stones. I find that straight up dumping them in the trash is a profoundly satisfying end to the spell, in a sort of 'this is what I think of your curse punk' kind of way.

Black Magick Variant – There are two ways to take the fight back into the teeth of the person(s) or spirit(s) that took a magical shot at you. The first is if you know who/where your enemy is, and burying the filled hematite stones within their magical perimeter (someone's yard, a spirits grave yard or building, etc). The second is to take a hammer (carved with runes or symbols of your intent to attack them) and smash the filled stones to pieces. With both spell variants you are filling the spells with your intent to do your enemy an equal harm as they attempted upon you. I call it the 'return to sender' spell, and if you want to 'put some pepper on it' then add the energy of your own outrage and feelings of revenge to the spell. An even more explicitly malevolent method of creating this curse is to perform hematite healing on other people, with the express intent of charging up your curse to place on someone.

Door Guardians

This is a spell with so many variants it is impossible to list them all, and to list even a few would take up the rest of the book, so I will choose the two that resonates with me. The idea here is that you are using a physical item to either create or invite a spirit (usually) or deity (or some sliver of that deity) to occupy a guardian position at the threshold of your home. The concept of thresholds is cross-cultural, and another element of the occult that is so potent that it has become commonplace in conventional culture. Some of you may wish to craft a servitor (referenced in prior chapter) while others may wish to craft items that will invite specific existing spirits or deities to stand the watch. I will detail the creation of a servitor I use called simply "The Warrior" who protects my home from outside the threshold, and I will go into the Loa Skull that I keep inside the threshold, which draws up on the Vodoun loa spirit of Papa Legba.

Materials - The Warrior (plaster garden statue, clay offering bowl) and Loa Skull (resin human skull, large wooden bowl, two large candles)

Execution - For The Warrior I procured a plaster garden statue (easily found at local statuary or some of the more interesting landscaping/garden stores) of a Roman Soldier. I placed the statue in the shade of a small tree on the side of my back yard, a good vantage point where he can see the whole property. I spoke the name I chose for him(which I'm not telling you!) over and over as I set the statue in place and positioned the clay bowl at his feet. I sat next to him and we shared a bottle of wine (he got most of it, which was only right), and as his cup ran over it soaked into the ground around him. I

filled the wine and my words with
his name and the purpose he was
being crafted to perform. Now that
he is active I occasionally will go
place various offerings in his
bowl, just to keep his batteries
full (as it were). The intent was
that he protected, aggressively,
our property from the outside. He
pings on malicious intent and
malevolent energy, and is built to
drive away the energy and to send
warnings if the threat is physical,
if not also lend his energy towards
what physical deterrents he might
be able to manifest (lots of zone
of probability inherent in his
weapons). For the Loa Skull I
bought a resin human skull, painted
the veve (a symbol) of Papa Legba
upon its forehead, and set it into
the bottom of the wooden bowl. The
skull has some space between it and
the bottom of the bowl, which is
covered in a layer of wax that
flowed from the two candles I lit
and held over the bowl as I invited
the loa Papa Legba to open a door
in the skull between himself and my
home. I regularly make Monday
offerings of rum by pouring it into

the bowl (the wax allows rum to disappear without soaking into the bowl and rotting it out). When I feel that the loa is working overtime or just wants more than rum I light a cigar and place it in the skull's lips (I remove it before it burns down to the point that it would melt the skull's teeth). This skull is set up BEHIND the front door, the idea being that Papa Legba isn't going to let anyone, anything, or any energy past the threshold that isn't good for the house and the occupants within. As I said, these are just two examples that I personally use as guardians, you should find what works for you. Maybe you would rather a Medusa door-knocker (the Aegis is a powerful symbol from Greek myth), or Fu dog statues on either side of the door, perhaps you'd rather carve symbols into the door and not bother with all of this statue/offering nonsense. This is up to you, and whatever works best for you is what will offer you the best protection.

Barbed Decoy

This spell flies in the face of much conventional wisdom with regards to the use of your own hair, teeth, nails, and blood, though it is the very potency of these things that give this spell its tremendous power. Around the world it is believed that parts of our body, once removed, can be used to form a connection with our true selves and allow spells to be cast with much more effective outcomes. Now that you are versed in the zones of connection and life force, you can see just how powerful those notions truly are, perhaps even more so when taken in context to yourself. The barbed decoy is a spell designed to act much like any other decoy you may have encountered in life, whether those are plastic animals used in hunting, multiple vehicles used in a smuggling scenario, or even the 'hat on a stick' trick used in cartoons and some films. The 'barbed' element comes from the incorporation of items that have a symbolic or literal 'thorny' implication, making your decoy similar in a way to the cactus or rose plants.

Materials - sealable glass jar (available at most hobby or craft stores), a sample of as much of your body as you are willing to provide (strand of hair, drop of blood, nail clippings, lost tooth, spittle, etc), thorns or nails as you are able (I tend to pick the spines from cactus plants when I'm building one, as I re-build mine anytime I move from one home to another)

Execution - Cleanse the jar as best you can, not only with hot water and soap but also energetically cleansing it with either a sage smudge (known to dispel any/all energy, even if the new age types often argue it just removes negative energy, sage is actually more of a hard energetic re-boot) or at the very least a good 'energy blast' from yourself. Then fill the jar with all of the items that are from your body. Each time you place an item in the jar fill it with your intent to create a target that will draw any oncoming malevolent energy directed at you to itself. For every piece of yourself you place in the jar add a thorn, spine, or nail, with the intent towards deterring any would-be attackers from making the same attempt twice. Place the jar somewhere that it will not be disturbed, but also where it will be out of sight by you or anyone you live with. It is important that a level of secrecy be kept, to complete the energetic transference of that bullseye you may or may not have painted on you.

Black Magick Variant – Instead of thorns or spine use assorted violent items, like razor blades, bullets, or a small knife to fill your jar. This is in keeping with the afore mentioned 'return to sender' approach to protection, a 'counter-strike' if you will.

HEALING

Pentacle Alignment

The pentacle, or five-pointed star, is a potent symbol in many ancient and reconstructionist traditions, predominantly of European sources. That being said, this could potentially work for anyone who is open to the idea of the star encompassing the totality of the physical elements or the cardinal directions (including the observer for that fifth). Another way of thinking about this symbol could be the iconic Leonardo Da Vinci's "Vitruvian Man" drawing, which is easily found online if you type in the above title. It is a symbol that is meant to encompass 'all that is' both internally and externally, which makes it exceptionally powerful as a symbol used for healing work. This spell is designed to 're-align' your spiritual energies, with a mind towards using those freshly balanced energies to correct any physical ailments that may be causing you trouble. This spell is particularly effective in working with both pain and spiritual parasites, in addition to being an aide in working against depression and anxiety. As you will see this spell is intended to be cast by one person in service of another's need.

Materials – spool of red thread, basin in which to burn a fire, container of water

Execution – Visualize the pentacle's shape while measuring a person using the red thread. First measure from each foot to the opposite hand, and then from each foot to the head, and finally across the arms. This procedure will create a pentacle, and for more accuracy use scotch tape to hold the threads in place at each measuring point. The more exact you can be in both your measurements and your intent the better. Pay attention to the thread as you measure, and keep your mind and energetic senses open, as you may glean additional information about the problem as you go. Most patients are only half truthful about what is vexing them, so be sure to keep a wary eye on the thread so that you may better serve your patient. After the measurements are finished and the pentacle formed, cut the thread from the spool and place it in the burning basin. Burn the thread until it is simple ash, and then mix that ash with water from your vessel. Once the water and ash have fully mixed into a concoction that is sufficiently wet for the patient to drink (usually 1-2 cups to fully gather and dissipate the ash) while they (and you) visualize their maladies having gone up in flames and the cure (or simple relief) entering their bodies via the ash/water potion.

Citrus Mojo Sponge

This spell has its roots in ancient healing remedies, though is most easily recognizable as a benign holiday ornament. The clove-pierced citrus fruit, usually an orange or lemon, serves as a 'sponge' that, somewhat like a black hole or whirlpool, draws energy into it. This spell works as a sort of energy filter, only specifically created towards the purpose of scrubbing a home (or person) of a specific ailment. For this spell, like so many others, the intent and target of the spell must be as specific as possible in order to maximize the potency and effectiveness of the spell. In fact, the more foreknowledge of the spell that the target person(s) has the more powerful it can be. Much like the afore mentioned 'hematite' spell, the citrus fruit(s) could be filled with 'bad mojo' and need to be swapped out from time to time, depending on the severity of the malady.

Materials - At the market choose one or more of the most vital and healthy citrus fruits you are able to secure, in addition to dried cloves (which could be tricky depending on where you are shopping, but most groceries at least have bagged cloves), and the yarn can be had at just about any hobby store, use one citrus fruit for each door in the home in which the person resides, though you can just use one for the door to their bedroom (or wherever they sleep) if you are in a place with multitudes of individuals, a spool of red yard from the local hobby store

Execution - Name the person you are casting the spell for and infuse the fruit with your intent as you pierce it with the cloves. Ideally you will only push the cloves in deep enough to break the skin, without puncturing the fruit within. This is for two reasons, the first being that if the meat is damaged the fruit will rot very quickly, and the second is that careful attention to each clove will keep your focus and intent sharp. The holes can be punched with the cloves themselves, or you can pre-punch the holes with a knife, ice pick, or large bore needle. Personally I find that the more steps to a spell the more powerful they perform for me, with specific regard to healing magick.

Something about the multiple steps that appeals to and resonates with the western medicine part of my psyche. Once the fruit is filled with many cloves, the exact number being completely up to you, tie the fruit up with the yarn and hand it from the doorknob. It is important to hand this in the threshold of the room, because that is the natural 'checkpoint' as it were, for energy as it flows through the home and the residents within. Once the malady has been cured (or the fruit is full of bad mojo and needs to be replaced) carefully removed the fruit from the door and throw it away somewhere off the property.

Black Magick Variant – Take the filled citrus fruits and place them (or hurl them, for added effect) into (or against) the property of someone that you wish to transfer your maladies to. As with other spells, actively engaging in the healing or protection of others, but with the hidden intent of harvesting their pain/maladies for use in magical assault, is what makes this a black magick variant.

Coffee Therapy

This is an expressly contemporary spell, despite the fact that coffee has been something magicians and practitioners have been using for a long time. I say this because I cannot point you towards a specific tradition that employs 'coffee baths' in their magical workings, though I don't want to say either that I'm inventing this. Much like other magick this is something that I've simply come up with through a combination of experience and study, though mostly experience if truth be told. Coffee is a powerful substance, and not just as a stimulant for the modern working stiff. Coffee can be used as both a healing tonic that is imbibed as a potion or it can be used as an ingredient in a ritual bath. Both methods allow the practitioner to physically imbibe in the caffeine and anti-oxidants present in coffee, but also to draw into themselves the magick of the earth, the bean, and the symbolic potency of coffee itself.

Materials - coffee beans, grinder, brewing apparatus (drip coffee makers are fine, but I prefer the French press because it requires a more mindful approach to the making of the coffee)

Execution - Go to your local supermarket with a specific intent to find the coffee that most appropriately resonates with you as a 'healing bean'. This may sound silly, but let's look at it this way, would you feel more healing mojo from an "English toffee coconut explosion" sort of coffee or an "Ethiopian Dark Roast"? It is not an obvious answer, and that is the point. Some people will prefer (and get better results from) a double chocolate pizzazz blend than they might from a basic medium roast. It is all about what resonates with you, and the buying of the coffee is just as much part of the magick as grinding, brewing, or imbibing it is. Once you choose your coffee return home and brew it in your chosen fashion. If you are making a tonic with it, allow the coffee to cool and then drink one cup of it mixed with one cup of ice cold water, the entire time envisioning the tonic as filling your insides with the power of the bean (fueled by the ritual of creating the tonic itself). If you are making a bath with it then pour the piping hot coffee, one cup will do but the whole pot works if you feel so inclined, into a hot bath you have drawn while brewing the coffee. Soak in the bath until it cools, allowing your physical body (and subtle energetic bodies also) to soak in the potion you have intentionally created as a healing and reinvigorating magical ritual. Both of these methods will encourage your body to void its bowels, because that is another part of coffee's power, to encourage the body to get rid of waste and toxins. This will occur faster with the tonic, though the bath will get you there in time also. As you void continue to focus your magical will upon ridding yourself of the malady. I know it sounds hilarious (in a juvenile way) but when you are done, flush your problems away (or bury them if you are outdoors when you cast this spell).

Feed the Pain

The idea of incorporating magick into the act of cooking is nothing new, though indeed deserves a resurgence in our contemporary age of bland convenience. The act of cooking itself is exceptionally well suited to being laden with magickal activity. So much of the 'kitchen busy work' is similar to the crafting elements of magick. Instead of preparing spell candles or reciting magical verse (though you could do both while you cook for an extra energy boost) the cook is chopping ingredients, applying heat in order to affect a chemical change, and putting effort into creating a thing that they or others will ingest. If you step back from our modern attitudes about the service industry in general and restaurants in specific, consider just how much trust you are placing in the people who cook your food. People pour energy into the food they cook, even those who don't believe in magick, and a practitioner can train themselves to detect these delicate threads of power in what they eat. A line cook who is having a bad day might dump some of that negative energy into the food, and a waiter who is annoyed with an unruly or ungrateful table may serve up those plates laden with their own negative energy. Following this idea, much could be said about the modern world of machine-prepared fast food, disgruntled service workers, and assembly line style "fine dining" restaurants, though suffice it to say if you wish to maximize your food intake with regards to the energy that comes along with it, maybe cook at home more often. Now, with that little bit of diatribe out of the way, let us return to the spell, which in this case is kitchen magick being used to facilitate healing. The broad idea is that the cook prepares a dish (or several) for the afflicted, which upon eating and digesting will aide in the recovery from their particular malady.

Materials – kitchen, cooking equipment, ingredients

Execution – Perform thorough observation, analyzation, and adjustment spell creation phases with regards to the afflicted. Based upon what you find there, and what their particular tastes may be, determine what food you will prepare for the spell. In this sort of magick the food itself is not only the vehicle for the spell's magickal energy, but is also a physical component that should be strongly considered. Someone suffering from intense bowel issues might not need a spicy dish, though someone with a head cold might benefit greatly. Perhaps the afflicted is suffering from depression or anxiety, and based on what you observe about them you may choose to take them on a culinary journey that helps them engage their problems or you may simply help them forget their troubles for a short time, both have value. Modern medicine is a powerful thing, for the mind and the body, and food spells should be performed in conjunction with such contemporary medicinal techniques. While the food can certainly help with physical and mental maladies, kitchen magick is especially effective with energetic healing. Once you determine what sort of meal you are making, it is time to go shopping. Use the freshest ingredients you can find, not only for taste and health but also the more less the food has been process the more ripe for energetic infusion it is for your spell. As with other spells, turn the act of shopping into part of the ritual itself, and fill your search for ingredients with intent. Choose the ingredients that fit the recipe, but also specifically select the ones that resonate with a compatible and empowering energy. Some have said that 'food is alive, in a way, and wants to help' and based on my experience I am generally inclined to agree.

Prepare your kitchen for spellcraft by whatever means feel right to you. I personally play music that is of a similar vibration to the meal I am making, and (because I have an affinity for fire) I usually have one or more candles burning, each carved with symbols of the spell I am casting. As you serve up the food (perhaps on ritually oriented wares) continue to pour your energy and intent into the act of serving, so that you have applied your magical will to every aspect of the meal. Once the meal is over continue to keep your spell going, as now the act of cleaning the wares and the kitchen itself becomes the symbolic (and literal) act of cleansing the 'healing space'. You wash away the afflicting energy as you clean the kitchen space, and rid the home of whatever it was that the afflicted was suffering from.

Black Magick Variant – Cooking and serving food can be an effective and devious way of turning the act of cooking and serving food into a delivery system for hexes and curses. I know a waiter in Washington DC who works in a mid-range restaurant (that I will not name here) that casts spells on his customers using a ritual salt shaker he keeps in hit pocket. Nobody notices a few extra granules of salt on their meal do they? The waiter is a very politically active individual, and regularly cast spells to help or hinder politicians and lobbyists that he recognizes if they happen to dine at one of his tables. Trust is so important in food, and you are opening yourself up to the cook and the servers, for good or ill.

ATTACK

As a general approach towards terminology I tend to draw a distinction between a curse and a hex. In my thinking, and thus my individual practice, a curse is an attack spell that is more long lasting, something that may take a slower path towards the outcome. A hex, on the other hand, is a hard and fast 'one off' sort of attack spell. As such I believe that hexes are more direct, more detectable, and come packed with a tremendous amount of explosive power. The curse is a more subtle and insidious thing, slowly and surely working its way towards the malevolent outcome, and so curses can be more difficult for the enemy to detect. To put it another way, a hex might manifest as a terrible automobile collision, or a sudden heart attack, while a curse might manifest as an increasingly horrible run of bad luck, degrading health, financial ruin, etc. Unlike other spell groups I am only going to include two in this section, as a way of illustrating a classic hex and a classic curse, given the ultimate simplicity of creating attack spells. You should be able to take these two basic spells and remix them to serve your own ends. The 'why' behind casting these spells, and thus the resonance of your energy and the intent behind the spells, is the determining factor (in my thinking) of whether or not this is simple attack magick (magical violence) or actual black magick (malevolence). To bring things back to the fencing metaphor, the sword that takes a life in self-defense can be the same sword that takes a life in anger, the wielder's intent is what makes the violence one kind or another.

Candle Hex

This is a variation of the usual 'hoodoo' spells involving dolls, though oriented towards a swift and overwhelming single assault. The candle acts as something of a delivery system, like a firearm or longbow, and the pin-stuck symbols carved upon it are the projectiles. This is a spell for causing swift physical harm to your enemy, so this is the magick of broken bones, car crashes, and heart attacks.

Materials - large black candle, five needles

Execution - Carve five symbols or markings into the wax of the candle, evenly spacing them from the top of the candle to the bottom. I traditionally use a red candle for this activity, because of the symbolism inherent in the dripping red wax and the corresponding running blood of my enemy (zone of connection). You may choose to use any color, and I imagine a great many people may choose black, though I personally prefer red for hex work and black for curse work. The symbol can be runes, scribbles of your own design, or any kind of marking that symbolizes harm towards your enemy. After you have carved your marks fill each pin with your intent to do harm to your target, and as you let out a deep breath drive a pin through each of the symbols. Now that the candle is carved, pinned, and brimming with harmful energies, hold the thought of your enemy in mind and light the candle. As the candle burns down whisper your harmful intent and continue to feed the flames with your energy. When I do this spell there is no reason to not go all the way, and so I usually hold the candle in my hand, allowing the wax to flow where it will, which hurts, but that's just more energy for the spell. Once the flame dies the spell is cast.

Coffin Curse

This spell can be as disgusting as you are willing to make it, and the further you go the more powerful the curse will be. This is a spell that can be cast on an individual or group of targets as long as they share some common bond (like targeting all members of a corporate board, an enemy group of practitioners, a political administration, etc). The coffin has obvious symbolic connection to death and ruin, and this spell exacerbates that connection with famine and pestilence. Depending on your enemy it may or may not be possible to procure a piece of their physical selves (hair, skin, fingernails, etc) though thanks to the modern age of technology their photos can be had easily, possibly also physical address, place of work, etc. The more 'items of connection' that you can fill the coffin with the better, so that as you place the harmful items and refuse the spell can be more tightly focused. Because this is a curse the power of the spell will manifest itself over time as the toxicity of the coffin becomes mirrored by the lives of the enemy.

Materials – full size wooden coffin, though if you are not in a position to afford a coffin or have a place to store such a large piece a smaller once can certainly be used (often available online or at craft/hobby shops), physical or representative items of the target(s), physical items that represent harm, famine, disease, discomfort, and overall decay and ruin, etc (such as bullets, human waste, medical waste, rusted metal, broken glass, smashed dishes, ashes)

Execution – Prepare a space for the coffin by either making room in a storage closet, garage, or perhaps digging a hole in your private yard. Place the coffin in the space and fill it with all of the items representative of your enemy target as you focus your intent upon establishing a link between your coffin and the target. Next place several of your harmful items in the coffin, each time you place one fill it with your malice and intent to harm, perhaps even hurling the items into the coffin forcefully. Close the coffin lid and nail it shut, pushing more energy into the coffin as you hammer in the nails. If you use iron nails (which I recommend) then they will serve as a sort of protective 'grounding' defense for your curse, making it dramatically more difficult for your enemy to unravel the malevolent energies you have woven into their lives. By putting in the extra time and energy to create defenses for your curse the longevity of the spell is ensured. Ideally the coffin would be in an out of the way kind of place, especially if you are using any organic materials as part of your spell (blood, waste, etc). Personally I buried the coffin (mine was a simple coffin I built by hand using materials from the local hardware store), the one time I faced an enemy vile enough to warrant be casting such a spell. As the curse continues you are welcome and encouraged to pour more energy into your spell, perhaps add more harmful items, if the curse is taking an inordinate amount of time to manifest as fully and profoundly as you desire. Remember, curses take a long time, and have a more holistic (albeit negative) affect on the target, so be patient as the spell builds a manifestation momentum over time.

WIZARDS WITCHES EVERYWHERE

With spell casting being such a straightforward act, one might wonder why there are so many books on the subject. There are good reasons and not so good reasons.

On the not so good end, the truth is that a great many authors are simply cashing in on a perceived new age trend or witch craze, though once you have studied the magical arts at even a cursory level you will be able to see through these cheap charlatans and plastic shamans. If you bought this book instead of a Magical Seduction for Losers type booklet or some kind of Make A Magical Money Machine With Angel Power title then you've already successfully dodged the more obvious flotsam.

Sadly this kind of literary junk has become rather pervasive thanks to the advent of self-publishing, where anyone and everyone can slap together 20 pages of nonsense and throw it online.

The thing is, it works for those authors and finds a readership. Much of this material is on the bestseller list, which shows us that fancy covers and cool titles help sell books, and that a sucker is born every minute. To be fair, this volume is also a self-published book, with a catchy title and a cool cover, so it deserves the same scathing scrutiny from you that I just hurled at the afore mentioned hucksters.

The point I'm making is that there are vast stacks of books on the subject of casting spells and the occult overall, and that the majority of them are garbage. That's the not so good part.

The good part is that because there are so many books out there, even if ninety percent of them are trash, the ten percent that are good is still a sizeable stack of books.

There are upwards of one million new books published in the United States of America alone every year. That's a lot of books, so many in fact that none of us are going to be able to get around to reading them all. The great thing about this is that once you get handy as sifting through the trash to find the real winners, you'll have a stack of books that is bound to have a title or two that will truly resonate with you. Even though we are talking, in this book, about an eclectic occult magical path, there will always (likely) be one or two cultures or magical traditions that you'll be attracted to over the rest. You might still dip into the secondary and tertiary traditions you choose to investigate, but it is likely you will find one in particular that becomes your 'go to' paradigm.

Here's the real fun part: Fiction counts too.

Myths are just stories, and religions are collections of stories to which a group of people attach heavy significance. Magical traditions, most of them anyway, have their roots in myth, and so come from stories. Let us imagine a conjure woman digging in the dirt to find a specific root to make a poultice for someone in the village. She knows which roots to dig for because of a myth, a story that was taught to her, as it was taught to her teacher and that teacher's teacher. Onwards it goes, and so magical traditions flourish with story, and some even become the complex magical systems we know of today.

Think about all of the books and articles out there about the magical significance of colors, of plants, of stones, and remind yourself that at some point someone either made that up or was told by a spirit or god. Anyone who digs deep enough will find that stories are the only real evidence anyone has to point too as a source for belief. For those on the eclectic occult path, those beliefs are the tools of the trade, and by seeing that they are, at their core, the results of stories, we can expand our base of knowledge and source material. We can happily and legitimately include fictional elements in our personal traditions.

If you read a book on the brujo traditions of Mexico and it resonates with you, then dive in and get yourself educated on that system. The more immersed in that tradition you become the more you'll be able to identify the tools most useful to you. I am adamant about this when I teach people in person. You can't pick and choose elements from other traditions without first immersing yourself in those traditions, at least for a little while.

I am not going to try putting together an Icelandic spell for speaking with the dead until I've found a solid source (likely a book, but maybe a teacher) and really dug into that tradition. It comes back to causality. Maybe the reason the Icelandic sorcerers perform the ghost speaking spell the way that they do is because of a story about elves who will come eat your face off if you don't perform a particular element of the spell correctly. Basically I'm saying that if you buy a book on Icelandic sorcery and skip straight ahead to the ghost-speaking spell then you'll be clueless about why the stave has to be made out of rowan wood. You will have missed the part where it is explained that speaking this word or that word when you cast the spell is a direct request to the elves to help you cast your spell, and the rowan wood is how you protect yourself from them when they show up.

If you skip ahead you miss the story, and so you have no context in which to understand why you are doing what you are doing, and if you don't know why then it is tough to fully drive your energy and intent into a fully formed and functional spell.

When you mix and match and borrow from other cultures and traditions, it is on you to make sure you understand the context of what you are plucking up to place into your own work.

If the Icelandic sorcerers are using rowan wood for their staves, then there is a reason, and there is a story somewhere that explains what that reason is. If you can accomplish your goal using a patchwork spell of your own creation, then go for it, but if you are going to go all-in with a culture specific spell you are willingly participating in that culture, so know your sources.

Say it with me everyone… Know Your Sources.

Nothing says 'cultural appropriation' like having elves eat your face off because you skipped the basics.

MAGICK vs MAGICK

I was raised in a home with a somewhat eclectic spirituality, and they pulled from a multitude of cultures despite being somewhat Judeo-Christian in their worldview. Neither of them were overt practitioners of the magical arts in any sort of way that was steeped in any particular culture. My mother had Irish Catholic roots, blended with Welsh sin eater traditions and folklore, while my father was raised in a rural Church of Jesus Christ. They found themselves once they got out on their own, and in the 60's and 70's discovered much in the way of freedom and new kinds of spirituality as the domineering and austere American culture was shaken up. My mother wasn't much of a practitioner of anything, though my father certainly participated in what I'll call a primordial chaos current. He was into the idea of picking and choosing pieces of other cultures and traditions to knit together a patchwork tapestry of a magical practice. He learned much from the likes of Crowley, Gardner, Leary, and similar thinkers and writers. I was given access to the family library and told it was up to me to decide what I believed, and I wasn't told about magick until I finally asked.

    The point I am making is that I do not come from a long-standing magical tradition, you'll find no bloodline of witches in my family tree, and I didn't even know magick existed until I experienced it for myself in my late teens. As a sort of DYI practitioner not raised in any particular tradition, I am pre-disposed towards occult magick, sometimes referred to by some as chaos magick or eclectic magick, which for all intents and purposes is the idea that "beliefs are tools". If a belief is a tool, then it can be used when needed, and when not needed can rest safely in the toolbox. I believe in ghosts, spirits, gods, and goddesses, even though I am not a devotee of any particular religion. The specific advantage for me as a practitioner is that I can freely borrow from any culture or magical tradition without reservation or dissonance, because I see everything as fair game. If burning candles doesn't work for me then I don't bother, and if praying to Zeus isn't getting me the outcome I'm looking for then I can start talking with Baron Samedi without having to make a fuss about it. There is a power inherent in all of that freedom, though in my opinion it also has a steep "jack of all trades and master of none" inherent cost.

As someone who is free to pick and choose from any culture or tradition, to use beliefs as tools instead of disciplines, I will never be able to push as much power through those affectations as the people to whom they are not affectations at all, but articles of faith, belief, and tradition. People who are raised in or at the very least sincerely choose a specific magical tradition, or even a culture that includes a magical tradition of some kind even if they are not schooled in it until later in life, have the capacity for much more potent magical activity within the context of that culture and tradition.

For example: Let us suppose that for one reason or another I enter into a magical conflict with an avowed practitioner of hoodoo that also happens to be a devotee of Papa Ogun.

I personally have a strong resonance with Papa Ogun, who is a sort of warrior and healer deity within the Vodoun religion, though my connection with the loa (or spirit) would not be nearly as strong as a full devotee. As such, it would be unlikely that I would be able to entreat Ogun to move against that person. Certainly it would be possible for a power like that to be called down on both sides of a conflict, though in this specific instance I am just not bringing the same level of energetic connectivity to the war table as the devotee. My relationship with Ogun could prove ineffective at blocking hexes and otherwise bad mojo being cast against me by a devotee of the same loa. Nor would it be overly effective for me to use hoodoo to fight hoodoo, if my opponent is an avowed practitioner of hoodoo exclusively. That person would be steeped in hoodoo, and know intricacies of both spellcraft and spirit interactions specific to hoodoo that I would be clueless about.

    Being an occult sorcerer I have the option of drawing upon a vast array of other resources to engage in the conflict. Perhaps I would counter a hoodoo hex with an Icelandic rune stave or a Native American dream catcher, or even a full-fledged Hermetic Banishing ritual. All of those things are more likely to be effective in a struggle with a hoodoo practitioner than it would be for me to attempt spells with hoodoo resonance. In such a conflict I would observe that the context forces surrounding the hoodoo practitioner are likely sufficient that I would be ill advised to employ hoodoo against them, as in that specific endeavor their energetic momentum, or auric momentum as it were, would overpower mine, and any hoodoo I cast would be ineffectual at best and backfire at worst.

This is something very important for those of us who follow a more occult or eclectic path to remember. We are the more versatile swimmers in the vast ocean of light, but cultural practitioners are the apex predators of their chosen waters. Always be observant about where you are, who you are with, and what kind of energetic resonance dominates the landscape. There are obvious territories such as the American South for hoodoo and Vodoun, places such as the state of Florida or the nation of Cuba for Santeria, or the remote Netherlands for Norse sorcery, though there are pockets of culture and tradition throughout the world. As our planet becomes more globalized the more and more these cultures with magical traditions will be present.

That is a bounty in that those

of us with more fluid magical methods and ideas will have more access to vibrant cultures and magical traditions, yielding more 'belief tools' for our toolboxes, though we must also work to respect and nurture those cultures. Magick is all about causality remember? All of our awesome belief tools came from static cultures and rigid magical traditions, and we don't get to have tables of botanical associations, rune languages, or pantheons of gods and spirits without the (for lack of a better term) fundamentalists of those cultures and traditions. Respect the culture practitioner, even if they are unable or unwilling to engage with their belief as if it were a tool that could be picked up and set down, because you wouldn't have your own in the first place without the tradition that gave them theirs.

THE TOOLBOX

There are a great many sorts of highly specialized magick that I have not touched upon in this volume, and others which will only be given cursory discussion here, some with recommendations for books by other authors. These are areas of magick that while they can be positioned into the Prosperity, Healing, Protection, and Attack spell groups, they only do so in the broadest sense. No single magical system, as present by an individual teacher, group, or tradition, can possibly encompass all of the magickal techniques, beliefs, and spellcrafts that exist in this world (or have yet to be created by you, the reader).

My goal with this book has been and remains through to publication the presentation of a system that can be a foundation from which to build. There is a common saying that a home is only as strong as its foundation, and that, my friends, is what I am seeking to present you. As you delve into these specialized forms of magick with additional research and experimentation, thanks to your occult foundation, you can effectively incorporate elements of what you read below into your personal practice.

Angel & Demon Magick – There are a great many practitioners who rely (some exclusively) upon magick that draws its power from angels or demons. In some cases those practitioners even invoke (or evoke, depending on the spells) the divine/infernal presences of such beings, and through the use of ritual words and symbols manage to control them for a short time. If you wish to continue study in this vein there are an exhausting number of books available, though I find that those of the Thelemite tradition tend to have the most effective and empowered approach in this regard. I've seen Thelemites perform incredible feats of magick, and if you must pursue this path, I advise you start by contacting your local Ordo Templi Orientis organization and go from there. The book

Chaos Magick - There is no current in the occult world that is stronger or stranger than that of the chaos practitioners, often referred to as chaotes or discordians. Much like my eclectic occult system the chaotes are keenly interested in paradigm modeling and the borrowing of techniques from a multitude of cultures to craft individual magical systems. I personally do not affiliate with this current because along with the effective practitioners and spiritual pioneers the chaos current comes with a dearth of immature individuals with inordinate attachment to drug use, pop culture, and petty trolling. That being said, I find that practitioners of chaos magick often find much use in my occult magick system, even as I myself have been shaped in the past by my contact with chaos practitioners and their methodologies. To that end, I would recommend picking up the book

"Condensed Chaos" by Phil Hine for a somewhat academic journey into the current and "Chaos Magick" by Seth Cardorra for the more discordian path.

Necromancy - Death is a powerful force in the lives of we simple mortals, and as such there is an energy that resonates with death. There are death spirits and deities, from a multitude of traditions, that can be worked with directly, and most necromancy is based in dealings with external beings. There is no shortage of manuscripts detailing magical work with psychopomps (conductors of souls) from a variety of cultures, and often the dead themselves. Graveyards are obvious sources for energy that resonates with death energy, not to mention a wide selection of potential spirit allies or enemies. The same can be said for battlefields, haunted houses, hospitals, and major cities in general. The few necromancers I have had experiences with are predominantly concerned with crafting spells that allow them to communicate with the dead (to gain information or to banish them) and to offer protection for the perceived souls of the recently departed. You are able to incorporate necromancy (or death magick, as it were) into your work either by performing spellcraft while physically present in 'places of death' (like a graveyard) or securing an item that carries such resonance (coffin nail, grave dirt, bones, etc). Working in this way will give your death magick a resonance that will further empower your process, especially if you are attempting to work with a spirit, deity, or psychopomp.

Last, but not least, is the practice of 'ghost breaking', which is exorcism or banishment of harmful or otherwise malevolent ghosts, by another, more appropriate name. Necromancers, those practitioners who focus exclusively on death magick, are exceptional at communication with the dead, and so usually can coerce unruly ghosts to leave a haunting. For those of us who are not 'specialists' as it were, ghost breaking is an effective (even if energetically messy) method of stopping a malevolent haunting. It is Attack magick, and while there are an infinite number of ways to craft a breaker spell, here are two simple ways that have worked for me in the past. The first method is very direct, and used if you are able to find out who the harmful ghost is. Gather what items you can that are connected to this person, a photograph is the most direct, especially if it is an original and not something you downloaded off the internet (though that will work in a pinch). Boldly walk through the house calling out the name of the ghost, and once you've entered every room and walked down every hallway then go outside and circle the building once clockwise and once counterclockwise and make your way to the outside of the front door.

Place the photograph on the front door and hammer an iron nail through it as you repeat the words "I drive you out". The second method is for use when you have no clear idea who the ghost might be. The process is the same, walking through and around the building, though as you go this time carry a glass mason jar filled with salt water. Salt is often thought of in the same way that iron is, though specifically oriented towards dealing with spirits. As you walk keep the jar open, and visualize your magical will sweeping through the area and pushing all of the malevolent energy (and thus the presence that emanates the energy) into the jar. Once you make your rounds and reach the front door secure the lid of the jar and then set the jar on the ground just outside the property line. If the property line isn't clearly marked go into the street or alleyway and set the jar down there, the point is to get it away from the house or estate (or away from the entire apartment building and complex if you are working in a very urban environment). Shout "I drive you out!" and strike the top of the jar with a hammer as hard as you can, so that the jar shatters and spreads the water, thus dissipating the gathered energy and presence.

Wine Magick – There are several gods and goddesses, along with other spirits, that are associated with wine. Take Bacchus or Dionysus for example, who are Roman and Greek deities of the vine, respectively. One of the chief methods of communion with them is to imbibe ritually prepared wine from symbol-laden vessels. Speaking of communion, you also have the Eucharist ritual in the Christian faith, where again ritual wine is presented to those seeking (literally) a communion with their deity. What is often overlooked by re-constructionists of ancient faiths (especially neo-pagans who have an affinity for Dionysus) is that the wine cults of the ancient world were up to some very intense magick beyond simple devotional rituals. Dionysus was an Outsider god, the one who comes, and the use of the wine (for all its ritual pomp and circumstance) was secondary to the effect the wine had on the state of consciousness of the practitioners. It was the 'otherness' kind of altered state of consciousness that they were seeking, however as with most religions and long-standing traditions the ritual (or the tool) becomes the object of reverence, to the loss of the greater magick. This is how many of the wine cults of the ancient world (and some of the neo-pagan groups in our contemporary world) lost sight of the magical power available to them in this altered state of conscious made possible by the wine, and simply started to focus their worship and magical wills upon the wine itself. What I will call, for the sake of this text, wine magick, is all about re-capturing that empowered awareness of the power we can reap from altered states of consciousness. Wine is one of our oldest human inventions, and carries with it an energetic resonance of bounty, of ingenuity, and an inherent allure of sensation. It has always been an excellent symbolic stand-in for blood, and on the whole is a potent 'delivery system' for magical intent.

Incorporating wine into your spellcraft can modify the resonance of your work, giving it an edge of mystery, of earth, of prosperity, of vitality, and that heady sense of 'otherness' that so many practitioners already experience to one degree or another in their day-to-day lives. For the sake of responsible teaching, I do want to take a moment to specify that wine magick isn't 'drunk magick', and to attempt spellcraft while overly inebriated is inadvisable. With wine magick you are using the liquid in a 'materials' context, and even if you did imbibe you would be working towards that heady 'otherness' altered state of consciousness (which taken, in a ritual context, is easily achieved with one or two glasses for those with average body mass and tolerance for alcohol). Refer to my "Door Guardian" spell earlier in the book for an example of responsible wine magick. The caveat to that of course would be if you are intentionally planning to work with 'wine gods' such as Bacchus or Dionysus, in which case please drink plenty of water and consider the next morning's hangover as part of your willing sacrifice.

Blood Magick – This is a delicate subject for many people, including myself, for obvious reasons. Blood is often presented in our contemporary media as a material that gets regular use in spellcraft. There's always some busty witch cutting her palm or an evil wizard sacrificing someone on a big altar if you pay any attention to what is on television or in our games and comic books. The reality is somewhat less dramatic visually, though just as intense, if not more so, energetically. From my perspective blood is a powerful substance, and as such can be used to 'supercharge' any kind of spellcraft you might be engaged in. The method by which the blood is harvested, however, deeply affects the resonance of the energy it provides, so keep that in the front of your mind. There are only a handful of books on the subject, one is the "Blood Sorcery Bible" by Sorceress Cagliastro, and the other is simply "Blood Magick" by Seth Cardorra (though the blood magick material is also included in his Chaos Magick book, so it's pointless to buy both). To bring it back to my personal experience, I have occasionally used a clean needle to prick my fingertip, as that yields a fair amount of blood without much physical damage. I would not recommend doing much cutting, with razors or knives, because of the scarring factor, unless of course you are specifically intending to incorporate the scar tissue into long-term spellcraft.

Servitor Magick – If ever there was a 'hot topic' in the occult community it would be servitor magick, which put simply is a magical practice focused upon the creation of magickal entities. The general idea is that through spellcraft the practitioner is able to create an entity designed for either specific or broad arrays of functions. This topic truly does deserve its own book, as in many way it is a practice of 'occult robotics', complete with its own ethical conundrums concerning intentionally created self-aware entities or those who achieve self-awareness (and agency) on their own. Most of the servitors I have used in my own life have been simple 'drones' that perform a basic function and then dissipate, though there are plenty of magical 'gods & monsters' out there in a sort of Frankenstein type scenario, where practitioners have created incredibly powerful beings, some of which have broken free from their creators. For a good example of how I would make a servitor please refer to the "Door Guardian" spell in which I detail how I created 'The Warrior'. Granted, my warrior servitor (designed for protection) is bound in a physical object, this usually need not be the case. Most practitioners use symbols, generally unique ones crafted specifically for the entity being created, and that is sufficient for the extent of their tasks. People use them for all sorts of things, generally as single-use spells that continue auto-casting. Let's say you invest a few hundred (or thousand) dollars in an index fund on the stock market. As index funds are somewhat automated, and keep themselves balanced against the performance of the market, you may wish to create a servitor to 'manage' your portfolio. All this servitor would do is apply itself to your index fund, moving energy around amongst the different stocks in your portfolio (in actuality it is empowering the automated system that already does this). This sounds simple enough, and it is, until it is time for dividends to be paid out and your index fund has yielded (inexplicably) a few percentage points more than someone with the same automated fund. I could go on, but someone has already done a solid job of writing a servitor book. I recommend the book "Creating Magical Entities" by David Michael Cunningham. It might not have the same flashy covers and engaging buzzword titles that many other books have, especially the extra slim 'books' from 2014 and 2015, but it is the best piece I have found on the topic. In other words, Creating Magical Entities was written before the 'servitor craze' currently clogging up the various online retailers.

These are some, but by no means all, of the sorts of specialized magick you may encounter and choose to study further. Whatever you do, keep studying, keep learning. Continued education is the way to stay relevant and competitive in the realm of business, let it be so with the world of magick.

MAGICKAL COMPOST

This section is something of a catch all heap of ideas, scraps of wisdom, observations, ruminations, and assorted writings that didn't quite fit anywhere else. There is little in the way of organization in this section, please understand that going into it. I call this my magickal compost, because in the turning and churning of these fragments there is a fertile bounty to be realized.

Some of the most powerful moments of learning I have experienced came in the form of single paragraphs or tangential sentences, both online (forums and social media) and offline (books or scraps of conversation). Two exceptional books that have much to offer in this respect are "Arcane Lore" by Scribe 27 and "Cosmic Trigger" by Robert Anton Wilson.

What follows is the compost pile of assorted writings that I have been accruing during the process of writing this book and distilling my lifetime of magical experience into something coherent and useful to others.

Paradigm modeling is exactly what it sounds like, where you create your own belief systems at will, specifically geared towards what works for you. This will inform your spellcraft, because you will be borrowing from other traditions and worldviews in order to create your own, and as such it is important to have an understanding and respect for the cultures, traditions, and techniques which you are appropriating into your own modeling work.

Ethics is a tricky subject, especially when it comes to magick, though for the occult eclectic, I think it can be more on the simple side. Because we are coming from a position of using beliefs like tools, and not being bound to one religious belief or another, we have an opportunity to be somewhat objective in the judgment of our own actions and intentions. I say intentions very specifically, because it is my opinion that the tool is just a tool, and it is the willful intent behind the tool that is to be held responsible for the outcomes and consequences.

Again we are brought back to the metaphor of swordplay, and I would argue that the sword is not the bearer of the ethical values, but the bearer of the sword. By this logic I would also argue that offensive magick, such as curses, hexes, and the more "aggressive" methods of shielding (discussed elsewhere in this book), are not inherently capable of bearing judgment. Like the hurricane or earthquake, these magical powers are simply forces of nature acting within the world, it is in fact the intent of the sorcerer who bent those forces to his or her will upon whom the value judgment should be laid.

Astral projection is one of the

most difficult kinds of magick for me, or anyone really if they are being honest, to describe without relying almost exclusively on metaphor. Then again, in my way of working with occult magick, the use of metaphor is vital to the very act of astral projection, so get ready for lots of illustration. I really do see it like 'jacking into the matrix' and approach it much the same. Out of body experiences, astral projection, and avatar adventures in other worlds all has the sort of 'vision quest' potency to it, and so anything you experience out there consider to be worthy of consideration. Remember that you aren't just daydreaming, and we humans are not the only shapers of reality.

The magical resonance of places are important to take into account as you move through your empowered life. Though I have traveled abroad I can only speak to the energetic landscape of America with a degree of authority. As an American I am keenly aware of the blood-drenched history of my country, as well as the fact that nearly everyone here is part of an immigrant bloodline. We are the bastard wizards of a thousand traditions. America's energetic resonance is one that rewards bold action, and yet that fortune can be retracted in the blink of an eye, to be followed by epic ruin. I read once in Neil Gaiman's fiction novel "American Gods" that "America is a hard place for gods", and I find that to be true. Not just for gods, but human beings, spirits, practitioners, etc. This landscape is one of harsh beauty and costly bounty. For every lush forest there is a barren desert, and for every verdant spring there is a killing winter. Great empires of rail, glass, and steel have been built on the bones of former empires of dirt and stone. The glory and horror that forged our modern nation is present in all its people, none more so than the magical practitioners from here, as we are steeped in the energies of this land. We are misguided conquistador healers who can't seem to leave well enough alone, and there is both power and price in that truth. To be an occultist in America is to be able to tap into the epic power of glory and ruin that is inherent in this landscape. Look to your own lands, dear reader, and delve into the power you find there. While you may have an affinity for other places and energies, there is a definite pull towards the power of your birthplace. We grow by knowing where we come from, and over time the resonance of our own lives adds to the power of the landscape, so in our own small ways we change the world even as we are changed by it.

Sacred space is something that every human finds some use for, even if many people aren't fully aware of why they need it. Sacred space can potentially be found or created anywhere, and the truth is that all that IS is Sacred. However, we are simple human beings, and it is impossible for most of us to see the whole of reality as sacred space (even though it totally is). As such, we use our minds and our hands to create sacred spaces that our minds can fit into. We build temples, we grow sacred groves, and we revere (some of us do anyway) the great wonders of nature such as mountains, volcanoes, and ancient forests. Sacred space lends itself to magical activity, as the resonance of such places is already oriented towards the unseen and the divine.

There are, in my thinking, several sorts of sacred space that we humans can intentionally create. The first is the temporary space that we create ourselves, through acts of magick, small rituals, or group identity. Examples of this would be lighting a candle in a dark room, spray paint tagging a specific alley with symbols for use as ritual space, or the various gatherings, festivals, and group events that people attend. Another sort of sacred space, involving somewhat more effort and energy, is the 'inner sanctum'. This would be a specific room in a house or building that is expressly used as sacred space. In more modest homes this could even be a specific corner or section of a room, which works especially well for those who have children and need to maximize the useable square footage.

Thelemites are fond of keeping sanctums in their homes, or at least the home of one group member, as many of their rituals are highly theatrical and require much in the way of staging and props. The third is what most people initially think of, the temple or church, being an entire building or estate that has been dedicated as sacred space. Sadly there are few such massive sacred spaces for occultist, and by necessity (at least in America) we have become experts at making do with the temporary spaces we create on the fly or the scattered sanctums we either know of or are able to host ourselves. I highly recommend the book "Magic of the North Gate" by Josephine McCarthy as a reference for the building and maintenance of sacred space.

There is much power in academic study, as the more knowledge we unlock for ourselves the more ways we can draw the world unto us. To be the best practitioner you can be it is of absolute importance that we study everything we can get our hands on. Not at the expense of experience and living our lives, but we should fill much of our time with education, from books to lectures, to travel, museums, experience, movies, books, film, etc. The more of a wealth of knowledge we have to draw upon the more versatile we are when engaging our Spell Temple and the world at large.

In the ancient Greek world there was idea that our labor is sacred, the act of taking the raw elements of the world and making something useful with them. To provide that usefulness to the community was a powerful act, and in this way many of the old guilds of architects, builders, weavers, potters, blacksmiths, and such were in many way magical societies.

Sometimes they were expressly magical societies, ascribing much of their knowledge and power to gods or spirits in addition to their skill and strength as human beings. The root of this is something I would like to discuss, the idea that labor can be sacred, and with that in mind we can use the 'work of our hands' to further empower our spellcraft. By learning a trade or a skill, like carpentry, painting, sculpting, pottery, metal-working, leather working, weaving, knitting, bead work, or any other comparable medium we can use that expertise to fuel our magick.

If I am using a ritual knife in my spells, the spells become so much more powerful when the knife itself has been made by a practitioner, doubly so if that practitioner is me. I have met a knitting witch who casts spells using items of clothing she makes, and a close friend of mine uses his skills with a hacksaw and soldering iron to craft single-use spell vials and staves. Both of these individuals have experienced a higher degree of potency in their spellcraft once they achieved a mastery of a particular medium. Personally I am a painter, mostly acrylics, on plain canvas. While I may not be holding any gallery presentations or winning any awards soon, I have spent enough years learning brush technique and coloring that I can focus on my spellcraft while painting and produce functional spells while creating art. The idea here is that you become so adept at your medium that you can create and cast simultaneously, and each act empowers the other.

WHY MAGICK?

Something that I believe is often overlooked in magical texts, both historical and contemporary, is the strong consideration of our own motivations in striving for magical mastery. There are a great many reasons someone might take this journey, and in my thinking it is only right that there are a multitude, such is the vast mysterious adventure that is magic. There are, however, a handful of general motivations that I would like to touch upon, and a final 'unifying principle' that I have a personal belief in.

It is all well and good to seek power for its own sake, and I am certainly not the person to dissuade you from such a pursuit. There is a fierce and definite allure to simple self-improvement, and to transition from a curious dabbler to a seasoned practitioner is a valuable motivation indeed. Such a thing invites me to think of the multitudes of middle class Americans who flock to Krav Maga studios, Mixed Martial Arts programs, Kickboxing gyms, or any of the other various weekly combat activities. The average student of martial arts is not going to actually raise their fists and do violence upon another human being, though being physically and mentally prepared to do so provides those individuals with a confidence and poise that gives them a certain kind of power.

Studying physical combat, to carry this line of thinking a step further, also has the potential to instill a kind of humility in students whose egos are sufficiently balanced. When you know what can happen to people when they engage in violence, you are more empowered to make choices to engage or avoid such a scenario. It is also possible, depending on the individual, that others will sense this humility and power within you, and may find themselves considering the same possibilities. This can be applied to magick directly, in that if you have magick as yet another recourse in your metaphorical toolbox, and you are skilled in its use, then your course through life is forever changed by that. Once you have walked with gods and crossed curses with sorcerers you can't help but achieve some humility, because I promise you that victory isn't assured, and eventually you will lose. We take those losses and become improved by them, just like in any business or battle from conventional reality.

Let me give you a real world example from the workplace. Imagine for a moment that you are an employee who works in an office environment, perhaps in a commissioned sales capacity. In this scenario a great many obstacles could arise in your day to day. Perhaps you have a manager who is vindictive, a co-worker who is overly competitive, and are representing a product that is difficult to sell in the current economic climate. If you are 'just another working stiff' then your options for negotiating the troubled waters of office politics and tough economic times are somewhat slim. A practitioner of the magical arts has a vast array of additional tools to help them turn this scenario into something more sustainable. My point is that simply knowing you have tools on stand-by will give you a natural confidence that will yield the kind of critical thinking and calm response that will allow you to work with the problems without even using your magick to make life more quality.

Quality of life, now that we have arrived at this point, is generally the most fundamental motivation for the magical traditions that we have inherited from the practitioners of history.

Looking back through time we see that most of what we could call 'indigenous' traditions were rooted in making life better and easier for the people of the community. Whether that was a shaman interceding with a spirit on the behalf of a troubled villager, a root worker using her knowledge of magical and medicinal plants to heal someone, or the sorcerer who divides their time between setting curses on people and breaking curses others have set. So much of ancient magic was concerned with the same things we find ourselves looking to work with, because the day to day living that we do shapes who we are.

If you research into ancient magic you will find that much of it is focused upon things like healing, prosperity, attack, and protection. So much was this the focus that this is the fundamental categorization of my own spells. Practical application of magickal techniques is of paramount importance to me, and as such I am always looking for ways to illustrate this. As you continue in your journey you will begin to find that magick is at work in your life in ways large and small ALL THE TIME. Becoming aware of its ebb and flow will enable you to cast all of those spells, both large and small, that will yield a higher quality of life.

Let us return to our workplace scenario and look at what our options might be as practitioners.

So we are back at work, and you are dealing with the difficult manager, the competitive co-worker, and the down economy. If you are oriented towards increasing the overall positive vibrations of the world, then perhaps you would work to cast spells that would bring bounty and opportunity into the lives of your boss and co-worker. They could get promotions that send them to other offices or job offers that would take them out of your workplace entirely. If you are coming from a darker place (no judgment here) then you could use your magick to cause all manner of ills to befall them in such a way as to remove their influence on your life.

The key consideration for any magical act is that the resonance of what you DO with your magick has a way of building momentum that can become self-propagating. I am not saying that for every curse you cast you'll get cursed in return, and I am also not saying that for every blessing you dole out you'll get one put on you. I am pointing out that if you surround yourself with negative energy to the exclusion of the positive, then your world will be dark indeed. The same is said for positive energy, because in that scenario you will grow bored, weak, and eventually disappointed when the darkness inevitably returns. We all know you cannot have one without the other.

For each individual there will be a ratio of positive to negative, light to dark, giving to taking, and that is part of what makes life and magick such a grand adventure. You might cast a blessing on that workplace manager to get him or her out of your way, so that your rise within the company ranks has one less obstacle. While there was a blessing placed, it was for a selfish reason, and that is worth considering. To curse the manager out of your way is certainly an option, perhaps even the more obvious one, but in this scenario the blessing or the curse is laid upon the manager not for the manager's own good or ill, but for the selfish desires of the practitioner.

Too often in this world we are told that selfishness is something to be avoided, and yet nature rewards the selfish organism. Any act of magick is an act of selfishness, because YOU, the practitioner, are using your powers to alter the course of events in your life and the lives of others. You are changing how things are to how you want things to be, and there is a selfishness, perhaps even a divine arrogance, inherent in such an act of Will. Therein lies, in my thinking, the real understanding that the magical practitioner achieves which lies beyond the awareness of the uninitiated. Reality is a complicated and beautiful mess, a paradox of epic proportions, and we as practitioners are a reflection of that.

Beyond the basic motivations of

self-improvement and quality of life, in those of you for whom the above two things aren't quite enough, there is Reality at Large.

Take a moment and imagine that Reality (with a capital 'R' to denote all that we can measure, sense, or even imagine) is a multi-dimensional video game of vast complexity. For the purposes of this illustration we will consider that all sentient beings (as we understand sentience, which is likely very limited) are players in this immense game. If we think of ourselves as players moving through a vast world populated with other players, each with their own goals and destinies, we begin to see that every decision we make, large and small, has ripple effects, large and small, on the whole of Reality.

Taken in the largest possible context within the whole of the metaphorical game it is unlikely that anything we do will be of a great and lasting effect, though in a localized sense our actions matter tremendously. In this way I want you to take a moment to consider what kind of player you have been up to this point, and what kind of player you want to be going forward. I am not here to encourage you to be one kind of player or another, for the world needs The Good, The Bad, and The Neutral in equal measure. More that I am inviting you to consider that the kind of player you are will, in ways large and small, determine the sort of game world you inhabit now and in the future.

As you move through this game I would invite you to enjoy the adventure, to immerse yourself within the game, because as a practitioner you can see past the 'graphics' of the game and see the 'programming' of it. You have the unique ability to make changes in the game, bend some rules, break others, and maybe create a few of your own. In this metaphoric game you, as a practitioner, can make a conscious choice about what kind of player you are going to be. Are you a hero? A villain? Something else? Whatever you choose… be about it.

This video game metaphor translates to the real world by the practitioner demanding of themselves to live with purpose and tenacity. Use your magick to get what you Will, to be what you Will, to become who you Will.

Magick is a divine tool that can transform your life, your actions, and your self into the most potent versions of themselves.

Most importantly magick is about changing things, especially yourself.

That is, in my thinking, the greatest motivation of all.

Having the power to change reality at will.

Magick can change what is, affect what could be, and most of all empower you to Become.

THE AUTHOR

You are invited to get in touch with questions or comments by emailing me at thelornecross@gmail.com

For those of you that paid good money for this book I am deeply grateful for the purchase.

I hope you found this work to contain something of use to you, and wish you luck and power in your continued adventure.

CPSIA information can be obtained
at www.ICGtesting.com
Printed in the USA
LVOW12s1818230517
535559LV00006B/1154/P

9 781523 914951